Ancient Classics for English Readers

EDITED BY THE

REV. W. LUCAS COLLINS, M.A.

LUCIAN

CONTENTS OF THE SERIES.

LUCIAN

BY THE

REV. W. LUCAS COLLINS, M.A

AUTHOR OF

'ETONIANA,' 'THE PUBLIC SCHOOLS,' ETC.

PHILADELPHIA:

J. B. LIPPINCOTT COMPANY

CONTENTS.

LUCIAN.

CHAPTER I.

BIOGRAPHICAL.

LUCIAN (Lucianus, or Lycinus, as he sometimes calls himself) was born about A.D. 120, or perhaps a few years later, at Samosata, on the bank of the Euphrates, at that time the capital city of Commagene, and perhaps better known a century later from its heresiarch bishop, Paul. What we know of our author's life is chiefly gathered from incidental notices scattered through his numerous writings. Of his youthful days he has given what is probably a truthful account in a piece which he has entitled "The Dream." This appears to have been written in his successful later years (when men are most disposed to be open and honest about their early antecedents), and recited as a kind of prologue to his public readings of his works, before his fellow-citizens of Samosata. He tells us that his parents, who seem to have been in humble circumstances, held a council of the friends of the family to consult what should be done with their boy. They came to the conclusion that a liberal education was not to be thought of, because of the expense. The next best thing, for a lad who had already no doubt given token of some ability, was to choose some calling which should still be of an intellectual rather than a servile character. This is his own account of what took place in the family council:—

"When one proposed one thing and one another, according to their fancies or experience, my father turned to my maternal uncle — he was one of the party, and passed for an excellent carver of Mercuries *—'It is impossible,' said he, politely, 'in your presence, to give any other art the preference. So take this lad home with you, and teach him to be a good stone-cutter and statuary: for he has it in him, and is clever enough, as you know, with his hands.' He had formed this notion from the way in which I used to amuse myself in moulding wax. As soon as I left school, I used to scrape wax together, and make figures of oxen and horses, and men too, with some cleverness, as my father thought. This accomplishment had earned me many a beating from my schoolmasters; but at this moment it was praised as a sign of natural talent, and sanguine hopes were entertained that I should speedily become master of my new profession, from this early plastic fancy. So, on a day which was counted lucky for entering on my apprenticeship, to

* The figures of Mercury so commonly set up in the streets and at the gates of houses were mere busts without arms, and could not have required any very great amount of art in their production.

my uncle I was sent. I did not at all object to it myself: I thought I should find the work amusing enough, and be very proud when I could show my playmates how I could make gods, and cut out other little figures for myself and my special friends. But an accident happened to me, as is not uncommon with beginners. My uncle put a chisel in my hand, and bid me work it lightly over a slab of marble that lay in the shop, quoting at the same time the common proverb, 'Well begun is half done.' But, leaning too hard upon it, in my awkwardness, the slab broke; and my uncle, seizing a whip that lay at hand, made me pay my footing in no very gentle or encouraging fashion; so the first wages I earned were tears."

"I ran off straight home, sobbing and howling, with the tears running down my cheeks. I told them there all about the whip, and showed the wheals; and with loud complaints of my uncle's cruelty, I added that he had done it all out of envy,—because he was afraid I should soon make a better artist than himself. My mother was extremely indignant, and vented bitter reproaches against her brother." *

Of course, with the mother in such mood, we readily understand that young Lucian never went back to the shop. "I went to sleep," he says, "with my eyes full of tears, and that very night I had a dream." This dream, which the author goes on to relate, is a reproduction, adapted to suit the circumstances, of the well-known "Choice of Hercules." How far Lucian

* "The Dream," 2-4.

actually dreamed it, or thought he dreamed it, is impossible to say. He was imaginative enough, no doubt, to have pictured it all to himself in his sleep; or a youth who had hit upon so ingenious an explanation of his uncle's beating him was equally capable of inventing a dream for the family edification; or (and this is the most likely supposition) the practised fabulist might have only adopted it as an apposite parable for the audience before whom he related it. The dream was this: Two female figures seemed to have laid hold of him on either side, and struggled so fiercely for the possession that he felt as if he were being torn in two. "The one figure was of coarse and masculine aspect, with rough hair and callous hands, with her robe high-girt, and covered with dust—very like my uncle the stone-cutter when he was polishing his work; the other had a lovely face and graceful bearing, and was elegantly dressed." The first is "Statuary," who offers him, if he will follow her, an ample maintenance, good health, and possibly fame. He is not to be discouraged at her rough appearance; such, at first starting in life, were Phidias, Myron, and Praxiteles. The other graceful lady is "Liberal Education." She reminds him that he had already made some slight acquaintance with her: but much is still wanting. She will make her votary acquainted with all the noblest things which the noblest men in all times have done, and said, and written; she will adorn his soul with temperance, justice, gentleness, prudence, and fortitude; with the love of the beautiful, and the thirst for knowledge. Nay, she will give him that which all men covet—immortality. Her rival can but offer him the work and position of a mere labourer, earning his living by his hands, one of the vulgar herd, obliged to bow before his superiors, and working according to his patrons' taste.*

Lucian hardly waited, he says, for the termination of this divine creature's speech, before he sprang up, turned his back upon her rival, and threw himself into her embraces. "No doubt," he slyly observes, "the recollection of the flogging which my brief acquaintance with the other lady had got me the day before contributed not a little to my choice." The rejected claimant gnashed upon him savagely with her teeth, and then, "stiffening like a second Niobe," she was—very appropriately—turned into stone.†

Whatever truth there might be in the vision, Lucian's choice was made. How he found the means for the further education that was needful, we are not told; but he got himself trained in some way as a Rhetorician. That science was not only very popular, but its professors, when once they had made themselves a name, were pretty well paid. The Emperor Marcus Aurelius was himself a most liberal patron of this as of other sciences, and maintained public lectures on jurisprudence, with which rhetoric was directly connected, both at Rome and in the provinces.

* Wieland well remarks that the art of sculpture must have been very much on the decline, both in point of merit and reputation, to lead the writer to speak of it in such slighting terms.

† "The Dream," 6-14.

For some time after his education was completed, he seems to have wandered up and down Ionia, with very precarious means of support, exercising his profession, among other places, at Antioch, where he must have come into contact more or less with the new sect called "Christians,"—with what result we shall partly see hereafter. By degrees he got into some practice as an advocate: but not meeting with the success which he hoped for in that line, he took to composing orations for others to deliver, and to giving lectures upon rhetoric and the art of public speaking. In this latter capacity he travelled a good deal, as was the custom for all professors in those days, and delivered his lectures and declamations in the towns of Syria, Greece, Italy, and Gaul. It was in the last-named country—always a rich harvest-field, as we gather from Juvenal,* for travelling orators and lecturers on law—that he seems to have been most successful, and he continued there for ten years.

Whether he eventually grew tired of his profession, as some expressions in his writings would lead us to think, or whether he had made enough money by it to enable him to devote himself to the more strictly literary life to which his tastes and abilities alike pointed, —he gave up the study and the practice of Rhetoric in about his fortieth year. He cast off his old mistress, he says, because he had grown tired of her false ways: "she was always painting her face and tiring her head," and otherwise misbehaving herself, and he

* See his Satires, vii. 175, and xv. 111.

would endure it no longer. She had led him a very unquiet life of it, he declares, for some years. He makes poor Rhetoric, indeed, say in her defence in the same Dialogue, and with at least some degree of truth, that she had taken him up when he was young, poor, and unknown, had brought him fame and reputation, and lastly in Gaul had made him a wealthy man.* It is possible that the declining reputation in which the science, owing to the abuses introduced by unworthy professors, was beginning to be held throughout Greece, may have been one great reason for his withdrawing from it.

He delivered his last lecture on the subject at Thessalonica,—where he would again meet with, or at least hear something of, the members of the Christian Church. Thence he returned to his native town of Samosata, found his father still alive there,† and soon removed him and his whole family into Greece. He devoted the rest of his life to the study of philosophy and to his literary work, living in good style at Athens. It was here, as he tells us himself, that he got rid of his "barbarous Syrian speech," and perfected himself in that pure Attic diction which is marvellous in a writer who was virtually a foreigner. For such Greek as was spoken in Syria during the Empire was, as Lucian confesses, little better than a *patois*. To these years of his life at Athens are naturally assigned those Dialogues of his which have in them so much of the Aristophanic spirit and manner. There also he enjoyed

* "The Double Accusation," 27 and 31.
† "Alexander," 56.

the friendship of Demonax of Cyprus, who, if we may trust the character which his friend gives of him in the little biographical sketch which bears his name, well deserved to be called an eclectic philosopher. His philosophy, combining some of the highest tenets of the Socratic school with the contempt of riches and luxury affected by the Cynics, was, says Lucian, "mild, cheerful, and benevolent," and he lived respected to the end of his long life, "setting an example of moderation and wisdom to all who saw and heard him." *

Lucian still travelled occasionally, and on one occasion paid a visit to the reputed oracle of the arch-impostor Alexander, at Abonoteichos in Paphlagonia, of which he gives a very graphic account. This man exercised an extraordinary influence over the credulity not only of his own countrymen but of strangers

* Lucian gives us a number of conversational anecdotes of Demonax,—one of the few collections of classical ana. Perhaps the best is this. A certain sophist from Sidon, very fond of praising himself, was boasting that he understood all systems of philosophy. "If Aristotle calls me to the Lyceum, I can follow him: if Plato invites me to the Academy, I will meet him there: if Zeno to the Porch, I am ready: if Pythagoras calls upon me, I can be silent." Rising up quietly among the audience—"Hark!" said Demonax, addressing him—"Pythagoras calls you." There was evidently something in common between the two friends in their views upon religious questions. When a neighbour asked Demonax to accompany him to the temple of Æsculapius to pray for the recovery of his son, the philosopher replied—"Do you suppose that the god is deaf, that he cannot hear us where we are?"—Life of Demonax, 14, 27.

also. Lucian's zeal against such sham pretenders here brought him into some trouble, and went near to cost him his life. Alexander, who had specially invited him to an audience, held out his hand, according to custom, for his visitor to kiss; whereupon Lucian, by way of active protest against an imposture which he had already denounced, bit it so hard as actually to lame him for some time. The Prophet affected to treat the thing as a practical joke, but, when Lucian was leaving the country, gave private orders to the captain and crew of the vessel to fling the malicious unbeliever overboard—a fate which he only escaped through the unusual tender-heartedness of the Asiatic captain.

He seems to have become poorer again in his later years, and to have occasionally taken up his old profession. But at last the Emperor Marcus Aurelius (or, as Wieland rather thinks, Commodus) offered him an official appointment (something like that of Recorder, or Clerk of the Courts) at Alexandria in Egypt. His chief duties were, as he tells us, to preside over the courts of justice and to keep the records.* He thought it necessary to write an "Apology" for accepting this position; for it happened that he had just put forth an essay (which will come under notice hereafter) on the miseries of a state of dependence on great men, and was conscious that his enemies might take occasion to sneer at so stout a champion of independence thus consenting to sell himself for office. He must have felt like Dr Johnson when he consulted his friends as to the propriety of his accepting the

* "Apology," 12.

pension offered by Lord Bute, after the bitter definitions of the words "pension" and "pensioner" which he had given in the first edition of his Dictionary. The promotion did not come until, as he says, he "had one foot already in Charon's boat," for he must have been above seventy years old when he received it: but the emoluments were fairly good; he was allowed to perform the office by deputy, so that it did not interfere with his busy literary leisure at Athens, and he lived many years to enjoy it. He is said to have been a hundred years old when he died, but nothing certain is known of the date or manner of his death. It has been conjectured with much probability that in his later years he was troubled with the gout, a disorder to which he more than once makes allusion in his writings, very much in the tone of one who spoke from painful experience; and he has left two humorous mock-tragic dramatic scenes in which Gout is personified as the principal character. The torments of which she is the author to mankind are amusingly exaggerated. Philoctetes is made out to have been a sufferer, not from the bite of the snake or from the poisoned arrow, but simply from gout in his foot—enough to account for any amount of howls and lamentations, such as are put in his mouth by Sophocles; and Ulysses must have died by the same enemy, and not, as was fabled, by the poisonous spine of a sea-urchin.

It has been impossible, in the compass of this volume, even to notice all the works of this active and versatile writer, a descriptive catalogue of which would alone fill some pages. Nor has the common order of arrangement been here followed, but the Dialogues and other pieces have been grouped as seemed most convenient.

Though Lucian was always a popular writer, he has not found many modern translators. The formidable number of his works has no doubt been one reason for this. Spence's translation (1684) is termed by Dryden "scandalous." The version by "Eminent Hands," published in 1711, to which is prefixed a "Life" by Dryden, is very incorrect, though some of the pieces are rendered with considerable spirit. Tooke's translation (1820) is also full of the blunders of imperfect scholarship, though the English is often racy and good. Dr Franklin's is, on the whole, that which does most justice to the original. But no English translator approaches in point of excellence the admirable German version by Wieland.

CHAPTER II.

LUCIAN AND THE PAGAN OLYMPUS.

The best known and the most popular of our author's multifarious writings are his "Dialogues," many of which would form admirable dramatic scenes, containing more of the spirit of comedy, as we moderns understand it, than either the broad burlesque of Aristophanes or the somewhat sententious and didactic tone of Terence. The "Dialogues of the Gods," in which the old mythological deities are introduced to us as it were in undress, discussing their family affairs and private quarrels in the most familiar style, were composed with a double purpose by their writer. He not only seized upon the absurd points in religious fable as presenting excellent material for burlesque, but he indulged at the same time in the most caustic form of satire upon the popular belief, against which, long before his day, the intellect of even the heathen world had revolted. It is possible that his apprenticeship, brief as it was, to the manufacture of stone Mercuries helped to make him an iconoclast. The man who assists in the chiselling out of a god must know more or less that he "has a lie in his right hand." The unhesitating faith in which (apparently) he accepts the truth of all the popular legends about Jupiter and his court, treating them in the most matter-of-fact and earnest way, and assuming their literal truth in every detail, makes the satire all the more pungent. To have sifted the heap of legends into false and true, or to have explained that this was only a poetical illustration, or that an allegorical form of truth, would not have damaged the popular creed half so much as this representation of the Olympian deities under all the personal and domestic circumstances which followed, as necessary corollaries, from their supposed relations to each other. We need not wonder that the charge of atheism was hurled against him by all the defenders, honest or dishonest, of the national worship. Many as had been the blows struck against it by satirists and philosophers, Lucian's was, if not the hardest, the most deadly of all.

The Dialogue called "PROMETHEUS," though it stands alone, and is not classed among the "Dialogues of the Gods," is quite of the same character with these, and may be regarded as a kind of prologue to the series. As a punishment for the offence which he has given to Jupiter, Prometheus is being chained down upon Mount Caucasus, the idea of the scene being borrowed undoubtedly from the tragedy of Æschylus. The executioners of the punishment, however, in this case, are Vulcan and Mercury alone, without the aid of Strength and Force. The victim protests against the cruelty and injustice of his doom, and the mean and petty revenge taken by Jupiter (upon a deity of much older family than himself, too), just because he had been outwitted in the division of the sacrifice: for this he believes to have been the head and front of his offending.* What would be said of a mortal who should crucify his cook for tasting the soup, or cutting a bit off the roast? As for his creation of men,—the gods ought to be very much obliged to him: for where would be their temples, their honours and their sacrifices, if the earth had remained untenanted? Even the beauty of the universe would have had no admirers.† If it be said that these same mortals are wicked,—murderers, adulterers, and so forth,—the gods had better hold their tongues on that point, considering the examples set by themselves. Then, as to his gift of fire to men—it is mere envy in Jupiter to grudge it them; and gods ought surely to be widely beneficent, not envious and selfish. And, if the gods do not like to see fire used upon earth, at least they seem very much delighted with the smoke, when it comes up to them in the shape of incense. Mercury admits that his defence is, to say the least, very clever; but,

* Prometheus had cut up a victim, and divided the portions into two heaps, of which he gave Jupiter his choice. Jupiter chose that which seemed to have the best share of fat at the top, but found that beneath there was nothing but bones.

† " 'What use could the Deity have for man,' said Epicurus, 'that He should create him?' Surely, that there might be a being that could understand His works; that could have sense to admire and voice to proclaim His providence in arrangement, His plan of operation, His perfection in completing all." —Lactantius, Div. Instit., b. vii. c. 5.

he remarks, "you may think yourself very fortunate that Jupiter does not hear what you say, for he would surely send down a hundred vultures upon you instead of one."

The change of dynasty in heaven presents of course a salient point, here and elsewhere, to the satirist. He makes Prometheus in his agony appeal to the *ancient* deities,—Saturn, Jupiter, and Earth,—not recognising any of the new introductions. In this, too, he has followed Æschylus, who makes the great Titan call upon Earth and Sea and Air, to witness his treatment at the hands of a usurper.

Some of the shorter and more amusing of these "Dialogues of the Gods" are here given entire, and are a fair specimen of the humour of the rest.

JUPITER AND CUPID.

Cupid. Well, even if I have done wrong, pray forgive me, Jupiter; I am only a child, you see, and don't know any better.

Jupiter. Child, indeed, Master Cupid! you who are older than Iapetus! Because you don't happen to have grown a beard yet, and because your hair isn't grey, you are to be considered a child, I suppose—old and crafty as you are.

Cup. Why, what great harm have I done you—old as you say I am—that you should think of putting me in the stocks?

Jup. Look here, then, you mischievous imp! is this a trifle—the way in which you have disgraced me?

There is nothing you have not turned me into—satyr, bull, gold pieces, swan, eagle; but you never yet have made a single woman fall in love with me for myself, nor have I ever been able to make myself agreeable in any quarter in my own person, but I have to use magic in all such affairs, and disguise myself. And after all, it's the bull or the swan they fall in love with; if they see me, they die of terror.

Cup. Yes, no wonder; they are but mortal, you know, Jupiter, and can't endure your awful person.

Jup. How is it, then, that Apollo gets them to fall in love with him?

Cup. Well—Daphne, you know, ran away from him, for all his flowing locks and smooth face. But if you want to make yourself attractive, you mustn't shake your ægis, and carry your thunderbolt about with you, but make yourself look as pleasant as you can,—let your hair hang down on both sides of your face in curls,—put a fillet round it,—get a purple dress,—put on gilded sandals,—walk with the fashionable step, with a pipe and timbrel before you: you'll see, the women will run after you then, faster than the Mœnads do after Bacchus.

Jup. Away with you—I couldn't condescend to be attractive by making myself such a fool as that.

Cup. Very well, Jupiter, then give up love-making altogether; (*looking slyly at him*)—*that's* easy enough, you know.

Jup. Nay, I must go on with my courting, but you must find me some less troublesome fashion than that. And upon this sole condition, I let you off once more.

VULCAN AND APOLLO.

Vulcan. I say, Apollo—have you seen this young bantling that Maia has just produced? What a fine child it is!—smiles at everybody, and gives plain token already that it will turn out something wonderful—quite a blessing to us all.

Apollo. A blessing, you think, eh, Vulcan? that child—who is older, in point of wickedness, than old father Iapetus himself!

Vul. Why, what harm can a baby like that do to anybody?

Ap. Just ask Neptune,—he stole his trident. Or ask Mars,—the brat slipped his sword out of its sheath as quickly as you please; to say nothing of myself, and he has gone off with my bow and arrows.

Vul. What! that infant? who can hardly stand? the one in the cradle there?

Ap. You'll soon find out for yourself, Vulcan, if he pays you a visit.

Vul. Why, he has paid me a visit, just now.

Ap. Well, have you got all your tools safe? none of them missing, is there?

Vul. (*looking round*). No — they are all right, Apollo.

Ap. Nay, look carefully.

Vul. By Jove! I can't see my anvil!

Ap. You'll find it somewhere in his cradle, I'll be bound.

Vul. Why, he's as handy with his fingers as if he had studied thieving before he was born!

Ap. Ah! you haven't heard him yet talking, as pert and as glib as may be. Why, he wants to run errands for us all! Yesterday, he challenged Cupid to wrestle with him, and tripped up both his legs in some way, and threw him in a second. Then, when we were all applauding him, and Venus was hugging him after his victory, he stole her cestus; and while Jupiter was laughing at that, he was off with his majesty's sceptre. Ay, and if the thunderbolt did not happen to be heavy, and considerably hot withal, he would have stolen that too.

Vul. You make the child out to be a prodigy.

Ap. Not only that—he knows music already.

Vul. How did he find that out?

Ap. He got hold of a dead tortoise somewhere, and made its shell into an instrument: fitted it with pins, and put a bridge to it, and stretched seven strings across it. Then he sang to it,—something really quite pretty, Vulcan, and in good tune: I was absolutely jealous of him, though, as you know, I have practised the lyre some time. Maia declares, too, that he never stays in heaven at night, but goes down into the Shades, out of curiosity—or to steal something there, most likely. He has got wings, too, and has made himself a rod of some miraculous power, by which he guides and conducts the dead below.

Vul. Oh, I gave him that, myself, for a toy.

Ap. So, in return, to show his gratitude, your anvil——

Vul. By the by, you remind me. I must go and look if I can find it, as you say, anywhere in his cradle.

JUPITER, ÆSCULAPIUS, AND HERCULES.

Jupiter. Be quiet, do, both of you—Hercules and Æsculapius—quarrelling with one another, just like mortals. It's really quite unseemly, this kind of conduct; not at all the thing in Olympian society.

Hercules. But do you mean to say, Jupiter, this apothecary fellow is to sit above me?

Æsculapius. Quite fair I should; I'm the better deity.

Herc. In what way, you staring ass? Because Jupiter struck you with his lightning for doing what you had no right to do, and now out of sheer pity has made you into an immortal?

Æsc. Have you forgot, Hercules, the bonfire that you made of yourself upon Mount Œta, that you taunt me with having been burnt?

Herc. Our lives were considerably different. I, the son of Jove, who undertook all those labours to benefit my generation, conquering monsters and punishing tyrants: while you went about like a vagabond, collecting roots, of some little use perhaps to dose a few sick folk, but never having done a single deed of valour.

Æsc. All very fine; when I healed your sores, sir, when you came up here the other day half roasted between the effects of the tunic and the fire together. Well, if I haven't done much, at least I was never a slave, as you were—never carded wool in Lydia in a woman's dress—never had my face slapped by

Omphale with her gilt slipper: and never went mad and killed my wife and children.

Herc. If you don't stop that abuse, sir, you'll pretty soon find out that your immortality is not of much use to you. I'll take and pitch you head-first out of heaven; and it will be more than Pæan himself can do to mend you when your skull's broken.

Jup. Stop! I tell you both again, and don't annoy the company, or I'll turn you both out of the hall. But it's quite fair, Hercules, that Æsculapius should sit above you—because he died first.

JUNO AND LATONA.

Juno (*meeting her rival with a disdainful half-bow*). A lovely pair of brats indeed, Latona, you have presented Jupiter with!

Latona (*with a sweeping curtsey*). Oh, we cannot all of us be expected, your majesty, to produce such a beauty as Vulcan!

Ju. (*rather disconcerted*). Well, lame as he is, he is very useful. He's a charming artist, and has decorated heaven for us with excellent taste. Then he has married Venus, and she is wonderfully fond of him too. But those children of yours—why, that girl's quite a masculine creature, only fit for the country. And now this last expedition of hers into Scythia—everybody knows her horrible way of living there—killing her visitors and eating them—as bad as those cannibals, the Scythians themselves. Then Apollo,—he pretends, I'm told, to know everything

—archery, and music, and medicine, and magic to boot; and has set up his prophecy-shops, one at Delphi, and one in Claros, and one at Didymœ; and cheats the people who come to consult him, with his enigmas and *double-entendres*, which can be turned into answers to the question both ways, so that he can never be proved wrong. He makes it pay, no doubt; there are always fools enough in the world ready to be cheated by a fortune-teller. But wiser persons see through him well enough, for all his humbugging prodigies. Prophet as he is, he could not divine that he was to kill his favourite with a quoit; or foresee that Daphne would run away from him, in spite of his pretty face and his curls. I don't see, for my own part, how you could have been considered more fortunate in your children than poor Niobe.

La. Oh yes; I know how you hate to see my two darlings—the cannibal and the charlatan, as you are pleased to call them—in the company of the gods: especially when her beauty is the subject of remark, or when he plays after dinner, to the admiration of everybody.

Ju. Really, Latona, you make me laugh. Admire his playing indeed! Why, if the Muses had only thought proper to decide fairly, Marsyas ought to have skinned *him*, for he was unquestionably the better musician of the two. As it was, poor fellow, he was cheated, and lost his life by their unjust verdict. And as for your beautiful daughter,—yes, she was so beautiful, that when she knew she had been spied by Actæon, for fear that the young man should publish her ugliness, she set the dogs at him. And I might add that her occupation as a midwife is not over-maidenly.

La. You are mighty proud, Juno, because you are the consort of Jove, and so think you can insult us all as much as you please. But it will not be very long before I shall see you in your usual hysterics, when his majesty goes down to earth in disguise upon one of his intriguing rambles.

VENUS AND CUPID.

Venus. How in the world is it, Cupid, that you, who have mastered all the other gods, Jupiter and Neptune and Apollo and Rhea—and even me, your mother—yet you never try your hand upon Minerva? In her case, your torch seems to lose its fire, your quiver has no arrows, and your skill and cunning is all at fault.

Cupid. I am afraid of her, mother; she has such a terrible look, and such stern eyes, and is so horribly man-like. Whenever I bend my bow and take aim at her, she shakes her crest at me and frightens me so that I absolutely shake, and the arrow drops out of my hands.

Ven. But was not Mars even more terrible? Yet you disarmed and conquered him.

Cup. Oh, he gives in to me of his own accord, and invites me to attack him. But Minerva always eyes me suspiciously, and whenever I fly near her with my torch, "If you dare to touch me," she says, "I swear by my father, I'll run my spear through you, or take you by the leg and pitch you into Tartarus, or tear you limb from limb." She has often threatened me so; and then she looks so savage, and has got a horrible head of some kind fixed upon her breast, with snakes for hair, which I am dreadfully afraid of. It terrifies me, and I run away whenever I see it.

Ven. You are afraid of Minerva and her Gorgon, you say—you, who are not afraid of Jupiter's thunder-bolt! And pray, why are the Muses still untouched, as if they were out of the reach of your arrows? Do they shake their crests too, or do they display any Gorgon's heads?

Cup. Oh, mother! I should be ashamed to meddle with them—they are such respectable and dignified young ladies, always deep in their studies, or busy with their music; I often stand listening to them till I quite forget myself.

Ven. Well, let them alone; they *are* very respectable. But Diana, now—why do you never aim a shaft at her?

Cup. The fact is, I can't catch her; she is always flying over the mountains; besides, she has a little private love-affair of her own already.

Ven. With whom, child?

Cup. With the game—stags and fauns—that she hunts and brings down with her arrows; she cares for nothing else, that I know of. But as for that brother of hers, great archer as he is, and far as he is said to shoot——

Ven. (*laughing*). Yes, yes, I know, child—you've hit *him* often enough.

As a pendant to these "Dialogues of the Gods," though it is not one of the pieces which bear that name, we have an amusing satire, conceived in the same daring spirit of iconoclasm, called

JUPITER IN HEROICS.

The speculations of the rationalists of the day as to the existence or non-existence of the Olympian deities have reached the ears of Jupiter himself, and he enters upon the scene in a state of considerable excitement and indignation, marching up and down, and muttering, with a pallid face, and his skin the colour of a philosopher, to the great bewilderment of his family. He finds it impossible to give expression to his feelings in sober prose, but addresses Minerva in tragic verse, compounded from his recollections of Euripides. "Good heavens," says his goddess-daughter to herself, "what an awful prologue!" Not to show herself wanting in poetical taste, however, as indeed was due to her own reputation, she answers him in his own vein, in a cento from Homer. But, as the king of the gods is proceeding in the same strain, Juno comes upon the scene, and, like some mortal wives, has little sympathy with her husband's poetical vein. She begs him, for the sake of ordinary comprehensions, to confine himself to prose. "Remember, Jupiter," says she, "that all of us have not devoured Euripides bodily, as you have, and do not be angry if we are unable to keep up with you in this extempore tragedy." She draws her own conclusion at once as to the cause of this excitement. Plainly it is nothing more or less than a new love-affair. Jupiter scornfully assures her that this is quite a different matter. It is a question which concerns the honour and status of all the court of Olympus; men are actually discussing among themselves upon earth whether they shall hereafter do worship and sacrifice to the gods at all. A council of the immortals must be held at once on urgent affairs, although Minerva, with a cautious prudence which will always find imitators, suggests that it would be better to leave such questions to settle themselves, and that the safest way to treat scepticism is to ignore it. But her counsel is overruled, and Mercury has orders to summon a general assembly of the gods forthwith.

Mercury. O yes, O yes! the gods are to come to council immediately! No delay—all to be present—come, come! upon urgent affairs of state.

Jupiter. What! do you summon them in that bald, inartificial, prosaic fashion, Mercury—and on a business of such high importance?

Merc. Why, how would you have it done, then?

Jup. How would I have it done? I say, proclamation should be made in dignified style—in verse of some kind, and with a sort of poetical grandeur. They would be more likely to come.

Merc. Possibly. But that's the business of your epic poets and rhapsodists—I'm not at all poetical myself. I should infallibly spoil the job, by putting in a foot too much or a foot too little, and only get myself laughed at for my bungling poetry. I hear even Apollo himself ridiculed for some of his poetical oracles—though in his case obscurity covers a multitude of sins. Those who consult him have so much to do to make out his meaning that they haven't much leisure to criticise his verse.

Jup. Well, but, Mercury, mix up a little Homer in your summons—the form, you know, in which he used to call us together; you surely remember it.

Merc. Not very readily or clearly. However, I'll try :—

"Now, all ye female gods, and all ye male,
And all ye streams within old Ocean's pale,
And all ye nymphs, at Jove's high summons, come,
All ye who eat the sacred hecatomb !
Who sit and sniff the holy steam, come all,
Great names, and small names, and no names at all." *

Jup. Well done, Mercury ! a most admirable proclamation. Here they are all coming already. Now take and seat them, each in the order of their dignity —according to their material or their workmanship ; the golden ones in the first seats, the silver next to them ; then in succession those of ivory, brass, and stone,—and of these, let the works of Phidias, and Alcamenes, and Myron, and Euphranor, and suchlike artists, take precedence ; but let the rude and inartistic figures be pushed into some corner or other, just to fill up the meeting—and let them hold their tongues.

Merc. So be it ; they shall be seated according to their degree. But it may be as well for me to understand,—supposing one be of gold, weighing ever so

* A burlesque of sundry passages in Homer.

many talents, but not well executed, and altogether common and badly finished, is he to sit above the brazen statues of Myron and Polycleitus, or the marble of Phidias and Alcamenes? Or must I count the art as more worthy than the material?

Jup. It ought to be so, certainly; but we must give the gold the preference, all the same.

Merc. I understand. You would have me class them according to wealth, not according to merit or excellence. Now, then, you that are made of gold, here—in the first seats. (*Turning to Jupiter.*) It seems to me, your majesty, that the first places will be filled up entirely with barbarians. You see what the Greeks are—very graceful and beautiful, and of admirable workmanship, but of marble or brass, all of them, or even the most valuable, of ivory, with just a little gold to give them colour and brightness; while their interior is of wood, with probably a whole commonwealth of mice established inside them. Whereas that Bendis, and Anubis, and Atthis there, and Mēn, are of solid gold, and really of enormous value.*

Neptune (coming forward). And is this fair, Mercury, that this dog-faced monster from Egypt should sit above me—me—Neptune?

Merc. That's the rule. Because, my friend Earthshaker, Lysippus made you of brass, and consequently poor—the Corinthians having no gold at that time;

* Bendis was a Thracian goddess, in whom Herodotus recognises Diana. The Athenians had introduced her, and held a festival in her honour. Atthis and Mēn (Lunus) were Phrygian deities: Mithras was the Persian sun-god.

whereas that is the most valuable of all metals. You must make up your mind, therefore, to make room for him, and not be vexed about it; a god with a great gold nose like that must needs take precedence.

(*Enter* VENUS.)—*Ven.* (*coaxingly to Mercury*). Now then, Mercury dear, take and put me in a good place, please; I'm golden, you know.

Merc. Not at all, so far as I can see. Unless I'm very blind, you're cut out of white marble—from Pentelicus, I think—and it pleased Praxiteles to make a Venus of you, and hand you over to the people of Cnidus.

Ven. But I can produce a most unimpeachable witness—Homer himself. He continually calls me "golden Venus" all through his poems.

Merc. Yes; and the same authority calls Apollo "rich in gold" and "wealthy;" but you can see him sitting down there among the ordinary gods. He was stripped of his golden crown, you see, by the thieves, and they even stole the strings of his lyre. So you may think yourself well off that I don't put you down quite amongst the crowd.

(*Enter the* COLOSSUS *of* RHODES.)—*Col.* Now, who will venture to dispute precedence with me—me, who am the Sun, and of such a size to boot? If it had not been that the good people of Rhodes determined to construct me of extraordinary dimensions, they could have made sixteen golden gods for the same price.* Therefore I must be ranked higher, by the rule of

* Sixteen was the recognised number of legitimate gods.

proportion. Besides, look at the art and the workmanship,—so correct, though on such an immense scale.

Merc. What's to be done, Jupiter? It's a very hard question for me to decide. If I look at his material, he's only brass; but if I calculate how many talents' weight of brass he has in him, he's worth the most money of them all.

Jup. (*testily*). What the deuce does he want here at all—dwarfing all the rest of us into insignificance, as he does, and blocking up the meeting besides? (*Aloud to Colossus.*) Hark ye, good cousin of Rhodes, though you may be worth more than all these golden gods, how can you possibly take the highest seat, unless they all get up and you sit down by yourself? Why, one of your thighs would take up all the seats in the Pnyx! You'd better stand up, if you please,—and you can stoop your head a little towards the company.

Merc. Here's another difficulty, again. Here are two, both of brass, and of the same workmanship, both from the hands of Lysippus, and, more than all, equal in point of birth, both being sons of Jupiter—Bacchus, here, and Hercules. Which of them is to sit first? They're quarrelling over it, as you see.

Jup. We're wasting time, Mercury, when we ought to have begun business long ago. So let them sit down anyhow now, as they please. We will have another meeting hereafter about this question, and then I shall know better what regulations to make about precedence.

Merc. But, good heavens! what a row they all

make, shouting that perpetual cry, as they do,—"Divide, 'vide, 'vide the victims!" "Where's the nectar? where's the nectar?" "The ambrosia's all out! the ambrosia's all out!" "Where are the hecatombs? where are the hecatombs?" "Give us our share!"

Jup. Bid them hold their tongues, do, Mercury, that they may hear the object of the meeting, and let such nonsense alone.

Merc. But they don't all understand Greek, and I am no such universal linguist as to make proclamation in Scythian, and Persian, and Thracian, and Celtic. It will be best, I suppose, to make a motion with my hand for them to be silent.

Jup. Very well—do.

Merc. See, they're all as dumb as philosophers. Now's your time to speak. Do you see? they're all looking at you, waiting to hear what you're going to say.

Jup. (*clearing his throat*). Well, as you're my own son, Mercury, I don't mind telling you how I feel. You know how self-possessed and how eloquent I always am at public meetings?

Merc. I know I trembled whenever I heard you speak, especially when you used to threaten all that about wrenching up earth and sea from their foundations, you know, gods and all, and dangling that golden chain *——

* Lucian repeatedly brings forward, in these Dialogues, the gasconade which Homer put into the mouth of Jupiter, Il. viii. 18—

"A golden chain let down from heaven, and all,
Both gods and goddesses, your strength apply;

Jup. (*interrupting him*). But now, my son,—I can't tell whether it's the importance of the subject, or the vastness of the assembly (there are a tremendous lot of gods here, you see)—my ideas seem all in a whirl, and a sort of trembling has come over me, and my tongue seems as though it were tied. And the most unlucky thing of all is, I've forgotten the opening paragraph of my speech, which I had all ready prepared beforehand, that my exordium might be as attractive as possible.

Merc. Well, my good sir, you *are* in a bad way. They all mistrust your silence, and fancy they are to hear something very terrible, and that this is what makes you hesitate.

Jup. Suppose, Mercury, I were to rhapsodise a little,—that introduction, you know, out of Homer?

Merc. Which?

Jup. (*declaiming*)—

"Now, hear my words, ye gods and she-gods all——"

Merc. No—heaven forbid! you've given us enough of that stuff already. No—pray let that hackneyed style alone. Rather give them a bit out of one of the Philippics of Demosthenes—any one you please; you

Yet would ye fail to drag from heaven to earth,
Strive as ye may, your mighty master Jove:
But if I choose to make my power be known,
The earth itself and ocean I could raise,
And binding round Olympus' ridge the cord,
Leave them suspended so in middle air."—(Lord Derby.)

Jupiter here dislikes Mercury's allusion to it.

can alter and adapt it a little. That's the plan most of our modern orators adopt.

His Olympian majesty begins his oration, accordingly, with an adaptation of the opening of the First Philippic. But he presently descends to his own matter-of-fact style ("here," he says, "my Demosthenes fails me"), and relates how he had been present the day before, with some other gods, at a sacrifice of thanksgiving offered by a merchant-captain for his preservation from shipwreck—a very shabby affair, he complains it was, a single tough old cock for supper among sixteen gods. On his way home, he had heard two philosophers disputing, and, wishing to listen to their arguments, assumed a cloak and a long beard, and might, he declares, have very easily, for the nonce, passed for a philosopher himself. It was that rascal Damis the Epicurean, disputing with Timocles the Stoic, asserting that the gods took no heed to mortals or their affairs—in fact, practically denying their existence. Poor Timocles had been making a stout fight of it on the other side, but was so hard pressed by his opponent that Jupiter found him all in a perspiration and almost exhausted; he had therefore thrown the shadows of night round the disputants at once, and so put an end to the discussion. Following the crowd on their way home, he had been shocked to find that the majority were on the side of the atheistical Damis; and he had now summoned this assembly to take into their serious consideration the terrible results that would ensue if this opinion became the popular one.

No more victims, and gifts, and incense-offering,—"the gods may sit in heaven and starve." Damis and Timocles are to meet again, he understands, for public discussion, and Jupiter verily fears that unless the gods give some help to their own champion, the other will get the best of it. He begs that some one of the assembly will get up in his place and offer some advice. Mercury invites any "who are of the legal standing in point of age" (we are to understand there are a great many newly-introduced deities in the council) to rise and deliver his opinion.

To make the burlesque more complete, it is Momus, the jester of the Olympian conclave, who first rises in reply to Jupiter's invitation.* He has long expected this, and is not surprised at it. The gods have brought it upon themselves, by neglecting their duties notoriously. Here, among friends and gods, with no mortal to hear, he may venture to speak openly. Has Jupiter himself been careful to make distinction between the good and the evil upon earth? Has virtue found any reward, or vice any punishment? What have any of them been caring for but their victims and their dues? What shameful stories they have allowed the poets to tell of their private life!—stories which, he

* Lord Lyttelton, in his "Dialogues of the Dead," makes Lucian give his own explanation of this passage to Rabelais, who does not quite understand the introduction of Momus. "I think our priests admitted Momus into our heaven as the Indians are said to worship the Devil,—through fear. They had a mind to keep fair with him. For we may talk of the Giants as we will, but to our Gods there can be no enemy so formidable as he. Ridicule is the terror of all false religions."

admits, may possibly be true enough, yet not meet to be told to mortal hearers. And then the oracles, worse than vague, positively deceptive—witness those notorious productions of Apollo's about the empire which Crœsus was to destroy by crossing the Halys, and the sons of women who were to meet their fate at Salamis. No marvel if, when the gods are so remiss in their duties, men begin to grow tired of worshipping them.

Jupiter protests against such ribald language. He quotes his Demosthenes to the effect that it is much more easy to abuse and to find fault than to offer suggestions under difficulties.

Then Neptune asks leave to say a few words. He lives, indeed, at the bottom of the sea, and is not in the habit of interfering much in affairs on land, but he strongly advises that this Damis shall be silenced at once—by lightning, or some such irresistible argument. But Jupiter replies, very fairly, that this would only be a tacit admission on the part of the gods that they had no other kind of argument to offer. Apollo gives it as his opinion that the fault lies in Timocles himself, who, though a very sensible man, has not the knack of putting an argument clearly. Upon which Momus remarks that the recommendation of clearness and perspicuity certainly comes with a curious kind of propriety from Apollo, considering the style of his own oracular utterances. He invites him to give them an oracle now,—which of the two disputants will get the better in this contest? Apollo tries to excuse himself, on the ground that he has no tripod or incense, or other appliances at hand, and that he can do this kind of thing in much better style at Colophon or at Delphi. At last, urged by Jupiter to prove his art, and so put a stop to the jeers of Momus, he proceeds, with some apology for extempore versifying, to deliver an utterly incomprehensible oracle, which fully justifies the criticisms of his brother deity. Hercules offers to pull down the whole portico on the head of Damis, if the controversy should seem to be taking a turn unfavourable to the Olympian interests.

But now a messenger arrives from earth, no other than the brazen statue of Hermagoras—Mercury of the Forum—who stands in front of the Pœcile at Athens. He comes to announce—adopting the new fashion of heroics set by Jupiter—that the duel of the philosophers has been renewed. The gods agree to go down to see the battle, and the scene of the dialogue is supposed to change at once to Athens. There Timocles is trying to argue with his infidel opponent. He wonders, he says, that men do not stone him for his impious assertions. Damis does not see why men should take that trouble: the gods, if gods they be, can surely take their own part; they hear him, and yet they do not strike. But they will, replies Timocles; their vengeance is sure though slow. They are otherwise occupied, retorts the sceptic—gone out to dinner, perhaps, with those "blameless Ethiopians" —they often do, according to Homer; possibly, sometimes, even without waiting for an invitation. In vain does his opponent argue from the harmony and order of creation, and from the general consent of mankind: the very diversities of national worship, the many absurd forms of superstition, are claimed by his opponent as arguments on the other side. Timocles compares the world to a ship, which could not keep its course without a steersman. Damis replies that if there were, indeed, a divinity at the helm of this world's affairs, he would surely parcel out the duties of his crew better than he appears to do—putting the rascals and lubbers in command, and letting the best men be stowed away in holes and corners, and kept on short rations besides. Timocles, as a last resource, threatens to break the head of his opponent, who runs away laughing. Jupiter is in doubt, however, on which side the real victory lies. Mercury consoles him that the gods have still the majority on their side —three-fourths of the Greeks, all the rabble, and all the barbarians. "Nay, my son," replies Jupiter, "but that saying of Darius had much truth, which he uttered of his faithful general Zopyrus: I, too, had rather have one man like Damis on my side than ten thousand Babylonians." *

The satire, in its bold scepticism, seems to go much beyond the "Dialogues of the Gods." In those, it is but the absurdities of the popular mythology—always incredible, one cannot but think, to the educated intelligence—which he ridicules and exposes; a creed which, if it could be supposed to have any influence upon the moral conduct of men, could only have had an influence for evil. But in that which has now been sketched, he attacks the belief in a divine providence

* The story is told by Herodotus, iii. 154.

altogether: and though most of the arguments against such government of the world are chiefly taken from the manifest falsehood of certain items of the Greek popular creed, still the tone is too much that of pure materialism.

THE COUNCIL OF THE GODS.

In this amusing scene the absurdities of polytheism are put in the broadest light, and treated with the most admirable humour. The object of the Council, which is summoned by Jupiter's orders, is to institute a strict scrutiny into the right and title of the new gods—aliens and foreigners of all kinds and shapes—to a seat in the house of Olympus. They have lately found their way into heaven in such numbers that they are becoming quite a nuisance, as we have seen in the complaint made both by Neptune and Mercury in the dialogue just preceding.

Momus is again the chief spokesman; freedom of speech is, as he says, one of his main characteristics, and he is in the habit of giving his opinion without fear or favour. So, with Jupiter's permission, he will name some of what he considers the most gross cases of intrusion.

Momus. First, there is Bacchus; a grand pedigree his is!—half a mortal, not even a Greek by his mother's side, but the grandson of some Syro-Phœnician merchant-captain, Cadmus. Since he has been dignified with immortality, I shall say nothing about himself,—his style of head-dress, his drinking, or his unsteady gait. You can all see what he is, I suppose—more like a woman than a man, half crazy, and stinking of wine even before breakfast. But he has brought in his whole tribe to swell our company, and here he is with all his rout, whom he passes off as gods—Pan, and Silenus, and the Satyrs, a lot of rough country louts, goat-herds most of them, dancing-fellows, of all manner of strange shapes; one of them has horns, and is like a goat all below his waist, with a long beard—you hardly can tell him from a goat; another is a bald fellow with a flat nose, generally mounted on an ass—a Lydian, he is. Then there are the Satyrs with their little prick ears, bald too, they are, and with little budding horns like kids—Phrygians, I believe; and they've all got tails besides. You see the sort of gods my noble friend provides us with. And then we are surprised that men hold us in contempt, when they see such ridiculous and monstrous gods as these! I say nothing of his introducing two women here—one his mistress Ariadne (whose crown, too, he has put among the stars, forsooth!), and the other a farmer's daughter, Erigone. And what is more absurd than all, brother deities, he has brought her dog in too: for fear, I suppose, that the girl should cry if she hadn't her darling pet to keep her company in heaven. Now, don't you consider all this an insult,—mere drunken madness and absurdity? And now I'll tell you about one or two more.

Jupiter (*interrupting him*). Don't say a word, if you please, Momus, either about Hercules or Æsculapius—I see what you're driving at. As to those two, one is a physician, and cures diseases, and, as old Homer says, you know—"is worth a host of men;" and as to

Hercules,—why, he's my son, and earned his immortality by very hard work; so say no word against him.

Mom. Well, I'll hold my tongue, Jupiter, though I could say a good deal. They're both as black as cinders still, from the fire. If you would only give me leave to speak my mind freely, I've a good deal to say about you.

Jup. Oh, pray speak out, as far as I am concerned! Perhaps you charge me with being a foreigner too?

Mom. Well, in Crete they do say that, you know; and more than that, they show the place where you were buried. I don't believe them myself—any more than I do what the people of Ægium say,—that you are a changeling. But I do say this, that you've brought in too many of your illegitimate children here.

Momus goes on to tell the royal chairman some home truths, which Jupiter hears with great equanimity. Then he inveighs against the monstrous forms introduced from Eastern mythology; Phrygians and Medes like Atthis and Mithras, who cannot even talk Greek; the dog-faced Anubis, and the spotted bull from Memphis, apes and ibises from Egypt. And how can Jupiter himself have allowed them to put ram's horns on his head at Ammon? No wonder that mortals learn to despise him.

A solemn decree is drawn up by Momus, in strict legal form, beginning as follows: "Whereas divers aliens, not only Greeks but Barbarians, who are in no wise entitled to the freedom of our community, have got themselves enrolled as gods, and so crowded heaven that it has become a mere disorderly mob of all nations and languages: and whereas thereby the ambrosia and the nectar runs short, so that the latter is now four guineas a pint, because there are so many to drink it; and whereas these new-comers, in their impudence, push the old and real gods out of their places, and claim precedence for themselves, against all our ancient rights, and demand also priority of worship on earth; it seemed good, therefore, to the Senate and Commons of Olympus, to hold a High Court at the winter equinox, and to elect as Commissioners of Privileges seven of the greater gods,—three from the ancient council of the reign of Saturn, and four from the twelve gods, of whom Jupiter to be one."

The business of the Commission is to be the examination of all claims to a seat in Olympus. Claimants are to bring their witnesses, and prove their pure descent; and they who cannot make good their claims are to be sent back to the tombs of their fathers. Moreover, from this time forth every deity is to mind his or her proper business, and none to pursue more than one art or science; Minerva is not to practise physic, nor Æsculapius divination; and Apollo is to make his election, and either be a seer, or a musician, or a doctor—but not all three.

Jupiter had intended to put this decree to the vote; but, foreseeing that a great many who were there present would probably vote against it, he took the easier course of issuing it on his own royal authority.

The dramatic sketch entitled "Timon" handles the

Olympian Jupiter in the same free spirit as the preceding Dialogues, and is by some considered as the author's masterpiece. The character of Plutus, the god of Riches, introduced into the piece, is obviously borrowed from Aristophanes's comedy of that name. Timon is introduced after he has forsaken society, and is digging for his livelihood.

TIMON.

Timon (stopping his work, and leaning on his spade). O Jupiter!—god of Friendship, god of Hospitality, god of Sociality, god of the Hearth, Lightning-flasher, Oath-protector, Cloud-compeller, Thunderer,—or by whatever name those moon-struck poets please to call you (especially when they have a hitch in the verse, for then your great stock of titles helps to prop a lame line, or fill a gap in the metre),—where be your flashing lightnings now, and your rolling thunders, and that terrible levin-bolt of yours, blazing and red-hot? Plainly all these are nonsense,—a mere humbug of the poets, nothing but sonorous words. That thunderbolt which they are always singing of, that strikes so far and is so ready to hand,—it's quenched, I suppose? got cold, and hasn't a spark of fire left in it to scorch rascals. A man who has committed perjury is more afraid, now, of the snuff of last night's lamp than of your invincible lightning. 'Tis just as if you were to throw the stump of a torch among them,—they would have no fear of the fire or smoke, but only of getting besmirched with the black from it.

Ah, Jupiter! in your youthful days, when you were

hot-blooded and quick-tempered, then you used to deal summary justice against knaves and villains: never made truce with them for a day: but the lightning was always at work, and the ægis always shaking over them, and the thunder rolling, and the bolts continually launched here and there, like a skirmish of sharpshooters: and earthquakes shook us all like beans in a sieve, and snow came in heaps, and hail like pebbles, and—for I'm determined, you see, to speak my mind to you—then your rain was good strong rain,—each drop like a river. Why, in Deucalion's days, there rose such a deluge in no time, that everything was drowned except one little ark that stuck on Mount Lycôris, and preserved one little surviving spark of human life,—in order, I suppose, to breed a new generation worse than the other.

Well—you see the consequences of your laziness, and it serves you right. No man now offers you a sacrifice, or puts a garland on you, except at odd times the winners at Olympia; and they do it not because they feel under any obligation to do it, but merely in compliance with a kind of old custom. They'll very soon make you like Saturn, and take all your honours from you, though you think yourself the grandest of the gods. I say nothing as to how often they have robbed your temples—nay, some fellows, I hear, actually laid hands on your sacred person at Olympia; while you,—the great thunder-god,—did not even trouble yourself to set the dogs at them, or rouse the neighbours, but sat there quiet,—you, the celebrated Giant-killer and Titan-queller, as they call you,—while they cut your golden locks off your royal head, though you had a twenty-foot thunderbolt in your hand all the while. When does your High Mightiness mean to put a stop to all this which you are allowing to go on? How many conflagrations like Phaeton's, how many deluges like Deucalion's, does such a world as this deserve?

To pass now from public iniquities to my own case. After raising so many Athenians from poverty to wealth and greatness,—after helping every man that was in want—or rather, pouring my riches out wholesale to serve my friends,—when I have brought myself to poverty by this, these men utterly refuse to know me; men who used to honour me, worship me, hang on my very nod, now will not even look at me. If I meet any of them as I walk, they pass me without a glance, as though I were some old sepulchral stone fallen down through lapse of years: while those who see me in the distance turn into another path, as if I were some ill-omened vision which they feared to meet or look upon —I, who was so lately their benefactor and preserver!

So, in my distress, I have girt myself with skins, and retreated to this far corner; and here I dig the ground for four obols a day,—and talk philosophy to my spade and myself. One point I think I gain here; I shall no longer see the worthless in prosperity—for that were worse to bear than all. Now then, Son of Saturn and Rhea, wake up at last from this long deep slumber—for you've slept longer than Epimenides *—

* The Rip van Winkle of classic story. He is said to have sought shelter in a cave from the heat of the sun, while keep-

and blow your thunderbolt hot again, or heat it afresh in Ætna, and make it blaze lustily, and show a little righteous wrath, worthy of the Jove of younger days; unless, indeed, that be a true story which the Cretans tell, and you be dead and buried too.

Jupiter (in Olympus, disturbed by Timon's clamorous expostulations below). Who in the world, Mercury, is this fellow that's bawling so from Attica, down at the foot of Hymettus,—a perfect scarecrow, he looks, in a dirty goat-skin? Digging, I think he is, by his stooping posture. He's a very noisy impudent fellow. Some philosopher, I fancy, or he wouldn't use such blasphemous language.

Mercury. What do you say, father? don't you know Timon of Athens? He's the man who so often used to treat us with such magnificent sacrifices; that *nouveau riche*, you know, who used to offer whole hecatombs; at whose expense we were so splendidly entertained at the Diasia.

Jup. What a sad reverse of fortune! That fine, handsome, rich fellow, who had used to have such troops of friends round him! What has brought him to this?—so squalid and miserable, and having to dig for his bread, I suppose, by the way he drives his spade into the ground?

Mercury proceeds to inform his father that Timon's reckless generosity has reduced him to poverty, and that all the friends who shared his bounty have now

ing his father's sheep, and to have slept there for fifty-seven years.

deserted him. He has left the ungrateful city in disgust, and hired himself out as a day-labourer in the country. Jupiter, however, is not going to follow the example of mankind, and neglect the man from whom, in his day of prosperity, he has received so many favours. He is sorry that his case has hitherto escaped his notice; but really the noise and clamour those Athenians make with all their philosophical disputes has so disgusted him, that for some time he has not turned his eyes in their direction. "Go down to him at once," he says to Mercury, "and take Plutus with you, with a good supply of money; * and let Plutus take care not to leave him again so easily as he did before. As for those ungrateful friends of his, they shall have their deserts, as soon as ever I can get my lightning mended. I broke two of my strongest bolts the other day, launching them in a passion against Anaxagoras the Sophist, who was teaching his followers that we gods were an utter impossibility in the nature of things. I missed him (Pericles put his hand in the way),† and the lightning struck the temple of Castor, I am sorry to say, and destroyed it; but my bolt was all but shivered itself against the

* "Plutus, the god of gold,
Is but his steward."
—Shaksp., "Timon," act i. sc. 1.

The introduction of Plutus's name into this tragedy makes one curious to know whether the author was acquainted (through any translation) either with this dialogue of Lucian's or with the "Plutus" of Aristophanes.

† Anaxagoras, when accused of impiety and brought to trial, was protected by Pericles, who had been his pupil.

rock there. However, those rascals will be punished enough for the present, when they see Timon grown rich again."

Merc. See now, what a thing it is to make a clamour, and to be impudent and troublesome! I don't mean for lawyers only, but for those who put up prayers to heaven. Here's Timon going to be set up again as a rich man out of the extreme of poverty, all because of his noise and bold words attracting Jupiter's notice! If he had bent his back to his digging in silence, he might have dug on till doomsday without Jupiter's noticing him. (*He goes off, and returns with Plutus.*)

Plutus. I shan't go near that fellow, Jupiter.

Jup. How, my good Plutus,—not when I bid you?

Plu. No. He insulted me—turned me out of his house, and scattered me in all directions—me, the old friend of the family—all but pitched me out of doors, as if I burnt his fingers. What! go back to him, to be thrown to his parasites, and toadies, and harlots? No: send me to those who value the gift, who will make much of me, who honour me and desire my company; and let all those fools keep house still with Poverty, who prefer her to me. Let them get her to give them a spade and an old sheep-skin, and go dig for their twopence a-day, after squandering thousands in gifts to their friends.

Jup. Timon will never behave so to you again. His spade-husbandry will have taught him pretty well (unless his back's made of stuff that can't feel) that you are to be preferred to Poverty. You're rather a discontented personage, too: you blame Timon because he opened his doors and let you go where you liked, and neither locked you up nor watched you jealously; whereas at other times you cry out against the rich, saying that they confine you with bolts and bars, and put seals on you, so that you never get so much as a glimpse of daylight. You used to complain to me that you were suffocated in the dark holes they kept you in; and I must say you used to look quite pale and careworn, and your fingers quite contracted from the constant habit of counting; and you often threatened to escape from such confinement the moment you had a chance.

Plutus replies to Jupiter with some sensible remarks as to there being a mean between the prodigal and the miser; but he consents to pay Timon a visit at Jupiter's command, though feeling, as he says, that he might as well get into one of the Danaids' leaky water-jars, so sure is he to filter rapidly through the hands of such a master. The god of Riches, we must remember, is blind; and Mercury, who has to escort him to Athens, recommends him to hold fast by his coat-tail all the way down. Jupiter desires his messenger to call at Ætna on his way, and send up the Cyclops to mend his broken thunderbolt.

They find Timon hard at work, in the company of Poverty. But she has brought with her a band of other companions — Labour, and Perseverance, and Wisdom, and Fortitude. This is a stronger body-guard, as Mercury observes, than Plutus ever gathers round him. The god of Riches confesses it; he can be of no service to a man who has such friends about him, and he offers to begone at once. But Mercury reminds him of the will of Jove. Poverty pleads in vain that she has rescued him from his old associates, Sloth and Luxury, and is now forming him to virtue in her own more wholesome school; and though Timon asks with some roughness to be left still under her instruction, and bids Plutus begone "to make fools of other men as he has once of him," he is overruled by Mercury's appeal to his sense of gratitude to Jupiter, who has taken so much trouble to help him. Poverty reluctantly takes her leave, and with her depart Labour and Wisdom and the rest of her company.

Digging on in the earth by direction of Plutus, Timon finds an immense buried treasure, and the sight at once reawakens his love of riches. But it now takes another and more selfish form. Henceforth he will live for himself and not for others, and become the enemy of men as he had formerly been their injudicious friend. The name which he desires to be known by is that of "The Misanthrope." * The companions of his former days of splendour—who had been treated by him with such munificence, and had repaid him with such ingratitude—hear of his new wealth, and flock to him to make their excuses and apologies, to tender him all kinds of services, and to offer him public honours, if he will only give them a little of his new riches. Blows from his spade, and showers of stones, are his only answer. And in this

* "I am Misanthropos, and hate mankind."
—Shaksp., "Timon," act iv. sc. 3.

spirit the Dialogue (which concludes somewhat abruptly) leaves him.

Timon the Misanthrope was probably a real personage, round whose name many fictitious anecdotes gathered. Aristophanes refers to him more than once in his comedies as a well-known character; Plato mentions him, and, if we may trust Plutarch, he lived about the time of the Peloponnesian war. This latter writer speaks of his intimacy with the Cynic Apemantus, introduced in Shakspeare's play,* and gives us an anecdote of him in connection with Alcibiades. Apemantus, we are told, asked Timon why he so much affected the company of that young gallant, hating all other men as he professed to do? "Because," replied Timon, "I foresee that he shall one day become a great scourge to those I hate most—the Athenians."

* Shakspeare's play is founded chiefly on the twenty-eighth novel in Painter's "Palace of Pleasure."

CHAPTER III.

DIALOGUES OF THE DEAD.

Less original than the Olympian Dialogues,—for their idea must be allowed to be borrowed from Homer, while the inclination to moralise upon the vanity of earthly riches, and honours, and beauty, and the work of that great leveller Death, is common enough,—these have perhaps been even more popular. An imitation in great measure themselves, they have found imitators amongst the moderns, in their turn, who have shown considerable ability. The "Dialogues of the Dead" of Fontenelle and of Lord Lyttelton still find readers, and these imitations have charmed many to whom the original was unknown in any other way than by name.* The Dialogues of Fenelon, composed for the instruction of his pupil the Duke of Burgundy, were, again, an imitation of those of Fontenelle, but are somewhat more didactic, as we should expect, and less lively. But perhaps the most striking modern work for the

* "The dead," says Fontenelle in his preface, "ought to speak wisely, from their longer experience and greater leisure; it is to be hoped that they take rather more time to think than is usual with the living."

idea of which we are indebted to the Greek satirist is the 'Imaginary Conversations' of Walter Savage Landor.

Some three or four of the most striking of this series must content our readers here. The following, although it does not stand first in the common order of arrangement, seems to form the best introduction to the series.

CHARON AND HIS PASSENGERS.

Charon. Now listen to me, good people—I'll tell you how it is. The boat is but small, as you see, and somewhat rotten and leaky withal: and if the weight gets to one side, over we go: and here you are crowding in all at once, and with lots of luggage, every one of you. If you come on board here with all that lumber, I suspect you'll repent of it afterwards—especially those who can't swim.

Mercury. What's best for us to do then, to get safe across?

Cha. I'll tell you. You must all strip before you get in, and leave all those encumbrances on shore: and even then the boat will scarce hold you all. And you take care, Mercury, that no soul is admitted that is not in light marching order, and who has not left all his encumbrances, as I say, behind. Just stand at the gangway and overhaul them, and don't let them get in till they've stripped.

Merc. Quite right; I'll see to it.—Now, who comes first here?

Menippus. I—Menippus. Look—I've pitched my

wallet and staff into the lake; my coat, luckily, I didn't bring with me.

Merc. Get in, Menippus—you're a capital fellow. Take the best seat there, in the stern-sheets, next the steersman, and watch who gets on board.—Now, who's this fine gentleman?

Charmolaus. I'm Charmolaus of Megara—a general favourite. Many a lady would give fifty guineas for a kiss from me.

Merc. You'll have to leave your pretty face, and those valuable lips, and your long curls and smooth skin behind you, that's all. Ah! now you'll do—you're all right and tight now: get in.—But you, sir, there, in the purple and the diadem,—who are you?

Lampichus. Lampichus, king of Gelo.

Merc. And what d'ye mean by coming here with all that trumpery?

Lamp. How? Would it be seemly for a king to come here unrobed?

Merc. Well, for a king, perhaps not—but for a dead man, certainly. So put it all off.

Lamp. There—I've thrown my riches away.

Merc. Yes—and throw away your pride too, and your contempt for other people. You'll infallibly swamp the boat if you bring all that in.

Lamp. Just let me keep my diadem and mantle.

Merc. Impossible—off with them too.

Lamp. Well—anything more? because I've thrown them all off, as you see.

Merc. Your cruelty—and your folly—and your insolence—and bad temper—off with them all!

Lamp. There, then—I'm stripped entirely.

Merc. Very well—get in.—And you fat fellow, who aie you, with all that flesh on you?

Damasias. Damasias, the athlete.

Merc. Ay, you look like him: I remember having seen you in the games.

Dam. (*smiling*). Yes, Mercury; take me on board —I'm ready stripped, at any rate.

Merc. Stripped? Nay, my good sir, not with all that covering of flesh on you. You must get rid of that, or you'll sink the boat the moment you set your other foot in. And you must take off your garlands and trophies too.

Dam. Then—now I'm really stripped, and not heavier than these other dead gentlemen.

Merc. All right—the lighter the better: get in.

[In like manner the patrician has to lay aside his noble birth, his public honours, and statues, and testimonials—the very thought of them, Mercury declares, is enough to sink the boat; and the general is made to leave behind him all his victories and trophies—in the realms of the dead there is peace. Next comes the philosopher's turn.]

Merc. Who's this pompous and conceited personage, to judge from his looks—he with the knitted eyebrows there, and lost in meditation—that fellow with the long beard?

Men. One of those philosophers, Mercury—or rather those cheats and charlatans: make him strip too; you'll find some curious things hid under that cloak of his.

Merc. Take your habit off, to begin with, if you please — and now all that you have there, — great Jupiter! what a lot of humbug he was bringing with him—and ignorance, and disputatiousness, and vainglory, and useless questions, and prickly arguments, and involved statements,— ay, and wasted ingenuity, and solemn trifling, and quips and quirks of all kinds! Yes — by Jove! and there are gold pieces there, and impudence and luxury and debauchery—oh! I see them all, though you are trying to hide them! And your lies, and pomposity, and thinking yourself better than everybody else— away with all that, I say! Why, if you bring all that aboard, a fifty-oared galley wouldn't hold you!

Philosopher. Well, I'll leave it all behind then, if I must.

Men. But make him take his beard off too, Master Mercury; it's heavy and bushy, as you see; there's five pound weight of hair there, at the very least.

Merc. You're right. Take it off, sir!

Phil. But who is there who can shave me?

Merc. Menippus there will chop it off with the boat-hatchet—he can have the gunwale for a chopping-block.

Men. Nay, Mercury, lend us a saw—it will be more fun.

Merc. Oh, the hatchet will do! So—that's well; now you've got rid of your goatishness, you look something more like a man.

Men. Shall I chop a bit off his eyebrows as well?

Merc. By all means; he has stuck them up on his

forehead, to make himself look grander, I suppose. What's the matter now? You're crying, you rascal, are you—afraid of death? Make haste on board, will you?

Men. He's got something now under his arm.

Merc. What is it, Menippus?

Men. Flattery it is, Mercury—and a very profitable article he found it, while he was alive.

Philosopher (*in a fury*). And you, Menippus—leave your lawless tongue behind you, and your cursed independence, and mocking laugh; you're the only one of the party who dares laugh.

Merc. (*laughing*). No, no, Menippus -- they're very light, and take little room; besides, they are good things on a voyage. But you, Mr Orator there, throw away your rhetorical flourishes, and antitheses, and parallelisms, and barbarisms, and all that heavy wordy gear of yours.

Orator. There, then—there they go!

Merc. All right. Now then, slip the moorings. Haul that plank aboard—up anchor, and make sail. Mind your helm, master! And a good voyage to us!—What are you howling about, you fools? You, Philosopher, specially? Now that you've had your beard cropped?

Phil. Because, dear Mercury, I always thought the soul had been immortal.

Men. He's lying! It's something else that troubles him, most likely.

Merc. What's that?

Men. That he shall have no more expensive suppers

—nor, after spending all the night in debauchery, profess to lecture to the young men on moral philosophy in the morning, and take pay for it. That's what vexes him.

Phil. And you, Menippus—are you not sorry to die?

Men. How should I be, when I hastened to death without any call to it? But, while we are talking, don't you hear a noise as of some people shouting on the earth?

Merc. Yes, I do—and from more than one quarter. There's a public rejoicing yonder for the death of Lampichus; and the women have seized his wife, and the boys are stoning his children; and in Sicyon they are all praising Diophantus the orator for his funeral oration upon Crato here. Yes — and there is Damasias's mother wailing for him amongst her women. But there's not a soul weeping for you, Menippus—you're lying all alone.

Men. Not at all — you'll hear the dogs howling over me presently, and the ravens mournfully flapping their wings, when they gather to my funeral.

Merc. Stoutly said. But here we are at the landing-place. March off, all of you, to the judgment-seat straight; I and the ferryman must go and fetch a fresh batch.

Men. A pleasant trip to you, Mercury. So we'll be moving on. Come, what are you all dawdling for? You've got to be judged, you know; and the punishments, they tell me, are frightful—wheels, and stones, and vultures. Every man's life will be strictly inquired into, I can tell you.

The Cynic Menippus, introduced to us in this amusing dialogue,—"a dog of the real old breed," as Lucian calls him, "always ready to bark and bite"*— is a great favourite with the author, and reappears very frequently in these imaginary conversations. He was a disciple of Diogenes, and had been a usurer in earlier life, but having lost his wealth by the roguery of others, at last committed suicide. The banter with which he treats Charon in the little dialogue which follows is very humorous.

CHARON AND MENIPPUS.

Charon (calling after Menippus, who is walking off) Pay me your fare, you rascal!

Menippus. Bawl away, Charon, if it's any satisfaction to you.

Cha. Pay me, I say, for carrying you across!

Men. You can't get money from a man who hasn't got it.

Cha. Is there any man who has not got an obolus?

Men. I know nothing about anybody else; I know I haven't.

Cha. (catching hold of him). I'll strangle you, you villain! I will, by Pluto! if you don't pay.

Men. And I'll break your head with my staff.

Cha. Do you suppose you are to have such a long trip for nothing?

* The term "Cynic," applied to that school of philosophy, is derived from the Greek for "dog."

Men. Let Mercury pay for me, then; it was he put me on board.

Mercury. A very profitable job for me, by Jove! if I'm to pay for all the dead people.

Cha. (*to Men*). I shan't let you go.

Men. You can haul your boat ashore, then, for that matter, and wait as long as you please; but I don't see how you can take from me what I don't possess.

Cha. Didn't you know you had to pay it?

Men. I knew well enough; but I tell you I hadn't got it. Is a man not to die because he has no money?

Cha. Are you to be the only man, then, who can boast that he has crossed the Styx gratis?

Men. Gratis? Not at all, my good friend,—when I baled the boat, and helped you with the oar, and was the only man on board that didn't howl.

Cha. That has nothing to do with the passage-money; you must pay your obolus. It's against all our rules to do otherwise.

Men. Then take me back to life again.

Cha. Yes—a fine proposal—that I may get a whipping from Æacus for it.

Men. Then don't bother.

Cha. Show me what you've got in your scrip there.

Men. Lentils, if you please, and a bit of supper for Hecate.

Cha. (*turning to Mercury in despair*). Where on earth did you bring this dog of a Cynic from, Mercury? —chattering, as he did, all the way across, cutting his jokes and laughing at the other passengers, and singing while they were all bemoaning themselves.

Merc. Didn't you know, Charon, who your passenger was? A most independent fellow, who cares for nobody. That's Menippus.

Cha. (shaking his fist at him as he moves off). Well, let me only catch you again!

Men. (looking back and laughing). Ay, *if* you catch me; but 'tis hardly likely, my good friend, that you'll have me for a passenger twice.

MERCURY AND CHARON SQUARING ACCOUNTS.

Mercury. Let us have a reckoning, if you please, Mr Ferryman, how much you owe me up to this present date, that we mayn't have a squabble hereafter about the items.

Charon. By all means, Mercury—nothing like being correct in such matters; it saves a world of unpleasantness.

Merc. I supplied an anchor to your order—twenty-five drachmæ.

Cha. That's very dear.

Merc. I vow to Pluto I gave five for it. And a row-lock thong—two obols.

Cha. Well, put down five drachmæ and two obols.

Merc. And a needle to mend the sail. Five obols I paid for that.

Cha. Well, put that much down too.

Merc. Then, there's the wax for caulking the seams of the boat that were open, and nails, and a rope to make halyards of,—two drachmæ altogether.

Cha. Ay; you bought those worth the money.

Merc. That's all, if I've not forgotten something in

my account. And now, when do you propose to pay me?

Cha. It's out of my power, Mercury, at this moment; but if a pestilence or a war should send people down here in considerable numbers, you can make a good thing of it then by a little cheating in the passage-money.

Merc. So I may go to sleep at present, and put up prayers for all kinds of horrible things to happen, that I may get my dues thereby?

Cha. I've no other way of paying you, Mercury, indeed. At present, as you see, very few come our way. It's a time of peace, you know.

Merc. Well, so much the better, even if I have to wait for my money a while. But those men in the good old times—ah! you remember, Charon, what fine fellows used to come here,—good warriors all, covered with blood and wounds, most of them! Now, 'tis either somebody who has been poisoned by his son or his wife, or with his limbs and carcase bloated by gluttony,—pale spiritless wretches all of them, not a whit like the others. Most of them come here owing to their attempts to overreach each other in money matters, it seems to me.

Cha. Why, money is certainly a very desirable thing.

Merc. Then don't think me unreasonable, if you please, if I look sharp after your little debt to me.

When the Cynic philosopher has been admitted

into the region of shadows, he makes himself very much at home there. In another of these dialogues he cross-examines all the officials whom he meets, with the air of a traveller anxious for information; and his caustic wit does not spare the dead a whit more than it had spared the living. He begs Æacus to show him some of "the lions" in this new region. He professes great surprise at seeing the figures which once were Agamemnon, Ajax, and Achilles, now mere bones and dust; and asks to be allowed just to give Sardanapalus, whom the Cynic hates especially for his luxury and debauchery, a slap in the face; but Æacus assures him that his skull is as brittle as a woman's. Even the wise men and philosophers, he finds, cut no better figure here. "Where is Socrates?" he asks his guide. "You see that bald man yonder?" says Æacus. "Why, they are all bald alike here," replies Menippus. "Him with the flat nose, I mean." "They've all flat noses," replies Menippus again, looking at the hollow skulls round him. But Socrates, hearing the inquiry, answers for himself; and the new-comer into the lower world is able to assure the great Athenian that all men now admit his claim to universal knowledge, which rests, in fact, on the one ground of being conscious that man knows really nothing. But he learns something more about the Master of the Sophists from a little dialogue which he has with Cerberus.

MENIPPUS AND CERBERUS.

Menippus. I say, Cerberus (I'm a kind of cousin

of yours, you know—they call me a dog), tell me, by the holy Styx, how did Socrates behave himself when he came down among ye? I suppose, as you're a divinity, you can not only bark, but talk like a human creature, if you like?

Cerberus (*growling*). Well, when he was some way off, he came on with a perfectly unmoved countenance, appearing to have no dread at all of death, and to wish to make that plain to those who stood outside the gates here. But when once he got within the archway of the Shades, and saw the gloom and darkness; and when, as he seemed to be lingering, I bit him on the foot (just to help the hemlock), and dragged him down, he shrieked out like a child, and began to lament over his family and all sorts of things.

Men. So the man was but a sophist after all, and had no real contempt for death?

Cerb. No; but when he saw it must come, he steeled himself to meet it, professing to suffer not unwillingly what he must needs have suffered anyhow, that so he might win the admiration of the bystanders. In short, I could tell you much the same story of all those kind of people: up to the gate they are stout-hearted and bold enough, but it is when they get within that the trial comes.

Men. And how did you think I behaved when I came down?

Cerb. You were the only man, Menippus, who behaved worthy of your profession—you and Diogenes before you. You both came here by no force or compulsion, but of your own accord, laughing all the way, and bidding the others who came with you howl and be hanged to them.

The reflections which Lucian has put into the mouth of the Cynic in the following brief dialogue are of a graver kind.

MENIPPUS AND MERCURY.

Menippus. I say, Mercury, where are all the handsome men and women? Come—show me about a little, I am quite a stranger here.

Mercury. I haven't time, really. But look yonder, on your right; there are Hyacinthus, and Narcissus, and Nireus, and Achilles,—and Tyro, and Helen, and Leda; and, in short, all the celebrated beauties.

Men. I can see nought but bones and bare skulls,—all very much alike.

Merc. Yet all the poets have gone into raptures about those very bones which you seem to look upon with such contempt.

Men. Anyway, show me Helen; for I should never be able to make her out from the rest.

Merc. This skull is Helen.*

Men. And it was for this that a thousand ships were manned from all Greece, and so many Greeks and Trojans died in battle, and so many towns were laid waste!

* "Now get you to my lady's chamber, and tell her, let her paint an inch thick, to this favour she must come."—Hamlet, act v. sc. 1

Merc. Ay, but you never saw the lady alive, Menippus, or you would surely have said with Homer,—

"No marvel Trojans and the well-armed Greeks
For such a woman should long toils endure:
Like the immortal goddesses is she." *

If one looks at withered flowers which have lost their colour, of course they seem to have no beauty; but when they are in bloom, and have all their natural tints, they are very beautiful to see.

Men. Still I do wonder, Mercury, that the Greeks should never have bethought themselves that they were quarrelling for a thing that was so short-lived, and would perish so soon.

Merc. I have really no leisure for moralising, my good Menippus. So pick out a spot for yourself, and lay yourself down quietly; I must go and fetch some more dead people.

DIOGENES AND MAUSOLUS.

Diogenes. Prithee, my Carian friend, why do you give yourself such airs, and claim precedence of all of us?

Mausolus. In the first place, my friend of Sinope, by reason of my royal estate; I was king of all Caria, ruled over much of Lydia, reduced several of the islands, advanced as far as Miletus, and subdued most part of Ionia. Then, because I was handsome and tall, and a good warrior. Most of all, because I have a magnificent monument set up over me at Halicar-

* Hom., Il. iii. 156.

nassus,—no man that ever died has the like; so beautifully is it finished, men and horses sculptured to the life out of the finest marble: you can scarce find even a temple like it. Don't you think I have a right to be proud of all this?

Diog. Because of your kingdom, you say?—and your fine person,—and the great weight of your tomb?

Maus. Yes; that is what I am proud of.

Diog. But, my handsome friend (ha-ha!), you haven't much left of that strength and beauty that you talk about. If we asked any one to decide between our claims to good looks, I don't see why they should prefer your skull to mine. Both of us are bald and naked,—both of us show our teeth a good deal,—neither of us have any eyes,—and our noses are both rather flat. The tomb, indeed, and the marble statues, the men of Halicarnassus may show to their visitors, and boast of them as ornaments of their land; but as to you, my good friend, I don't see what good your monument does *you:* unless you may say this—that you bear a greater weight upon you than I do, pressed down as you are by all those heavy stones.

Maus. Are none of my glories to profit me, then? And are Mausolus and Diogenes to stand here on equal terms?

Diog. No; not exactly equal, most excellent sir; not at all. Mausolus has to lament when he remembers his earthly lot, how happy he was,—and Diogenes can laugh at him. And Mausolus can say how he had the tomb built for him at Halicarnassus by his wife and sister; while Diogenes does not know—and does not care—whether his body had any burial at all, but can say that he left behind him the reputation among the wise of having lived a life worthy of a man, —a loftier monument, base Carian slave, than yours, and built on a far safer foundation.

In another dialogue Diogenes talks in the same strain to Alexander, and recommends the waters of Lethe as the only remedy for the sad regrets which those must feel, who have exchanged the glories of earth for the cold and dreary equality which reigns among the dead below—a passionless and objectless existence, in which none but the bitterest Cynic, who rejoices in the discomfiture of all earthly ambitions, can take any pleasure. So also Achilles, in a dialogue with the young Antilochus—a premature visitor to these gloomy regions—repeats the melancholy wish which Homer has put into his mouth in the Odyssey—

"Rather would I in the sun's warmth divine
Serve a poor churl who drags his days in grief,
Than the whole lordship of the dead were mine." *

Such is the tone of these Dialogues throughout,—a grim despair disclosing itself through their cynical levity. Whatever the "Elysian Fields" of the poets might be, the satirist gives us no glimpse of them. All whom the new visitors meet are in tears,—except the infants. In one scene, Diogenes remarks a poor decrepit old man weeping bitterly. To him, one

* Hom., Odyss. xi. (Worsley).

would think, the change could have been not so very sad. Was he a king on earth? No. Or a man of rank and wealth? "No," is the reply; "I was in my ninetieth year, and miserably poor; I had to earn my bread by fishing. I had no children to succour me, and I was lame and blind." "What!" says the philosopher, "in such a case, could you really wish to have life prolonged?" "Ay," replies the old fisherman, echoing the thought of the great Achilles—"Ay, life is sweet, and death terrible."

THE TYRANT.

Although this is not classed amongst the "Dialogues of the Dead," there seems no reason why it should not find a place among them. Charon and his ghostly freight are a favourite subject for Lucian's satire, and he has here introduced them again in a dramatic scene of considerably more length than any of the preceding. The sparkling humour of the introduction gives additional force to the serious moral of the close.

CHARON, CLOTHO, MERCURY, ETC.

Charon. Well, Clotho, here's the boat all a-taut, and everything ready for crossing; we've pumped out the water, and stepped the mast, and hoisted the sail—the oars are in their row-locks, and, so far as I am concerned, nothing hinders us from weighing anchor and setting off. And that Mercury is keeping me waiting—he ought to have been here long ago. The boat lies here empty still, you see, when we might have made three trips already to-day; and now it's almost evening, and we haven't earned a penny yet. And I know Pluto will think it's all my laziness, whereas the fault lies in quite another quarter. That blessed ghost-conductor of ours has been drinking the waters of Lethe himself, I suppose, and has forgot to come back. He's most likely wrestling with the young men, or playing on his lyre,—or holding an argument, to show his subtle wit. Or very possibly my gentleman is doing a little thieving somewhere on the road, for that's one of his many accomplishments. He takes considerable liberties with us, I must say, considering that he's half our servant.

Clotho. You don't know, Charon, but that he has been hindered in some way; Jupiter may have wanted him for some extra work up above; *he's* his master too, you see.*

Cha. But he has no right to get more than his share of work out of our common property, Clotho: *I* never keep him, when it's his time to go. But I know what it is; with us he gets nothing but asphodel, and libations, and salt-cake, and such funeral fare—all the rest is gloom, and fog, and darkness; while in heaven 'tis all brightness, and lots of ambrosia, and nectar in abundance; so I suppose he finds it pleasanter to spend his time up there. He flies away from here fast enough, as if he were escaping out of prison; but when the hour comes for him to return, he moves very leisurely, and takes his time on the road down.

* The many offices of Mercury were a favourite subject of jest with Aristophanes as well as with Lucian. Some figures of the god represented him with his face painted half black and half white, to signify his double occupation, above and below.

Clo. Don't put yourself in a passion, Charon; look, here he comes, close by, bringing a large company with him—driving them before him, I should rather say, with his rod, like a flock of goats. But what's this? I see one of the party with his hands tied, and another laughing, and another with a wallet on his back and a club in his hand, looking very savage, and hurrying the rest on. And don't you see how Mercury himself is actually running down with sweat, and how dusty his feet are; he's quite out of breath, panting, with his mouth open.—What's the matter, Mercury? What are you so hurried about? You seem quite done up.

(*Enter* MERCURY, *very hot, with a large company of Ghosts.*)

Merc. Matter, Clotho? Why, I've been hunting this runaway here, till I suppose you thought I had run away myself to-day, and deserted my ship.

Clo. Who is he? and what did he want to run away for?

Merc. That's plain enough—because he wanted to live a little longer. He's a king or a tyrant of some sort, and from what I can make out from his howlings and lamentations, he complains that he is being taken away from a position of great enjoyment.

Clo. So the fool tried to run away, did he?—when the thread of his life was already spun out!

Merc. *Tried* to run away, did you say? Why, unless that stout fellow there, he with the club, had helped me, so that we contrived between us to catch him and tie him, he would have got clean off. From the moment that Atropos handed him over to me, he did nothing but kick and struggle all the way, and stuck his heels in the ground, so that it was very hard to get him along. Then sometimes he would beg and pray me to let him go—just for a little bit—offering me ever so much money. But I, as was my duty, refused—especially as it was impossible. But when we got just to the entrance, and I was counting over the dead, as usual, to Æacus, and he was checking them off by the list which your sister had sent him, lo and behold! this rascal had got off somehow or other, and was missing. So there was one dead man short of the count. Æacus frowned at me awfully. "Don't try your cheating game here, Mercury," says he,—"it's quite enough to play such tricks up above; here in the Shades we keep strict accounts, and you can't humbug *us*. A thousand and four, you observe, my list has marked on it; and you come here bringing me one too few—unless you please to say that Atropos cheated *you* in the reckoning." I quite blushed at his words, and recollected at once what had happened on the road; and when I cast my eyes round and couldn't see that wretch, I knew he had escaped, and ran back after him all the way, towards daylight, and that excellent fellow there went with me, of his own accord; and by running like race-horses we caught him just at Tænarus * —so near he was getting away.

* At which spot there was one of the reputed descents to the Shades.

The Ferryman desires them to waste no more time now in chattering, and proposes to start at once. Clotho and Mercury count the dead into the boat. First, three hundred infants,—including those who have been deserted and exposed. Charon (who is still very cross) complains of them as "a cargo of very unripe fruit." Mercury next hands him in four hundred old people; "they are ripe enough," he observes, "at any rate—and some rotten." Seven have died for love—besides a great philosopher, who has killed himself for the sake of a good-for-nothing woman. Several have died of a fever—including the physician who attended them. Cyniscus, too, is there, the Cynic philosopher, who has been eating some of Hecate's supper, and a quantity of raw onions besides, and has died of indigestion. His only complaint is that he has been forgotten by the Fates, and allowed to live on earth so long.

Megapenthes, the tyrant, who has made such a determined attempt to escape on the road, entreats Clotho to let him go back to life—only for a little while, if it were but five days, just to finish his new house, and to give some directions to his wife about some money,—he will be sure to come down again soon. He tries in vain to bribe the Inexorable by offers of gold. Or, he will give his son, his only son, as a hostage. Clotho reminds him that his prayer used to be that this son might survive him. That *had* been his wish, he confesses; but now he knows better. Clotho bids him take comfort; his son will follow him here speedily; he will be put to death by the tyrant who succeeds. At least he desires to know how things will go after his death. He shall hear, though the information will hardly be pleasant. His statues will be thrown down and trampled on: his wife, who has already been faithless to him, will marry her lover: his daughter will go into slavery. In vain he begs for life, though the life be that of a slave. Mercury, with the help of Cyniscus, drives him into the boat, and threatens to tie him to the mast. At this moment a little figure rushes forward, and begs not to be left behind. It is Micyllus, a poor cobbler. He has not found life on earth altogether so pleasant, that he cares to continue it. "At the very first signal of Atropos," says he, "I jumped up gladly, threw away my knife and leather, and an old shoe I had in my hand, and without stopping even to put on my slippers or wash off the black from my face, followed her at once—or rather led the way. There was nothing to call me back. I had no tie to life,—neither land, nor houses, nor gold, nor precious furniture; no glory and no statues had I to leave behind. Indeed I like all your ways down below very much; there's equality for all, and no man is better than his neighbour; it all seems to me uncommonly pleasant. I suppose nobody calls in debts here, or pays taxes: above all, there is no cold in winter, no sickness, and no beatings from great people. Here all is peace, and conditions seem quite reversed; we poor laugh and are merry, while your rich men groan and howl." He is eager to be ferried over at once to that further shore; and when Charon sulkily declares there is no room in the boat for him, he strips and proposes to swim across the Styx; he shall get over that way perhaps as fast as they will. At last it is settled that he is to sit on the tyrant's back; "and kick him well," says Clotho. The Cynic now takes up the dialogue. He, like his fellow-philosopher Menippus, has no money to pay his passage.

Cyniscus. I'll tell you the plain truth, Charon—I haven't a penny to pay for my passage: nothing in the world but my scrip and staff here. But I'm quite ready to pump or to row: you shall have no reason to complain, if you can find me a good strong oar.

Charon. Pull away, then. I must be content to get that much out of you.

Cyn. Shall I give you a song?

Cha. Well, do; if you know a good sea-stave.

Cyn. I know plenty, Charon. But these fellows are blubbering so loud, they'll drown my voice.

Dead men, in discordant chorus. O my riches!—O my lands!—Oh, what a beautiful house I've left behind me!—Alas! for all the money my heir will squander!—Alas, my poor dear children!—Ah! who'll gather the grapes from those vines I planted last year?

Merc. Have you nothing to lament, Micyllus? Indeed it's against all rule for any one to make this voyage without a few tears.

Micyllus. Nonsense! I've nothing to cry for, on such a pleasant voyage.

Merc. Nay, just cry a little, do—just to keep up the custom.

Mic. Very well, if you wish it, Mercury—here goes.—O my leather-parings! O my old shoes! Alas!

no longer shall I go from dawn till evening without food, nor walk barefoot and half-clad all the winter, with my teeth chattering for cold! And, oh dear! who will inherit my old awl and scraper?

Merc. There, that'll do; we've almost got across.

Cha. Now, pay your fares, all of you, the first thing. You there, fork out! And you! Now I've got all, I think.—Micyllus, where's your penny?

Mic. You joke, my friend; you might as well try to get blood out of a turnip, as they say, as money out of Micyllus. Heaven help me if I know a penny by sight—whether it's round or square!

The scene which follows, satire though it be, has a terrible amount of truth in it. The tone of burlesque passes almost into that of tragedy. It reads like a passage from some dramatic mediæval sermon. The dead are summoned one by one before the tribunal of Rhadamanthus. Each has to strip for examination: for, burnt in upon the breast of every man, patent now to the Judge of Souls, though invisible to mortal eyes, will be found the marks left by the sins of his past life.* Cyniscus presents himself first, cheerfully and confidently. Some faint indications there are upon

* This is from Plato. In his 'Gorgias' (524) Rhadamanthus finds the soul of the tyrant "full of the prints and scars of perjuries and wrongs which have been stamped there by each action." Tacitus (Ann. vi. 6), speaking of Tiberius, introduces the idea as that of Socrates: "If the minds of tyrants could be laid open to view, scars and wounds would be discovered upon them: since the mind is lacerated by cruelty, lust, and evil passions, even as the body is by stripes and blows."

his person of scars, healed over and almost obliterated. He explains that these are the traces of great faults committed in his youth through ignorance, which by the help of philosophy he has amended in his maturer years. He is acquitted, and bid to take his place among the just, after he shall have given evidence against the tyrant Megapenthes. Micyllus, the poor cobbler, who has had few temptations, shows no marks at all. But when Megapenthes, hanging back in terror from the scrutiny, is hurled by Tisiphone into the presence of the judge, Cyniscus has a terrible list of crimes to charge against him. He has abused his power and wealth to the most atrocious deeds of lust and cruelty. In vain he tries to deny the accusations: his Bed and his Lamp, the unwilling witnesses of his debaucheries, are summoned, by a bold and striking figure of impersonation, to bear their evidence against him; and when he is stripped for examination, his whole person is found to be livid with the marks imprinted on it by his crimes. The only question is what punishment shall be assigned him. The Cynic philosopher begs to suggest a new and fitting one.

Cyniscus. It is the custom, I believe, for all your dead here to drink the water of Lethe?

Rhadamanthus. Certainly.

Cyn. Then let this man alone not be permitted to taste it.

Rhad. And why so?

Cyn. So shall he suffer the bitterest punishment in the recollection of all that he has been and done, and all the power he had while on earth, and in the thought of his past pleasures.

Rhad. Excellently well advised ! Sentence is passed. Let him be fettered and carried away to Tartarus, there to remember all his past life.

The keen intellect which rejected, as some of the greatest minds of antiquity had done before him, the inventions of poet and mythologist as to the future state, could appreciate the awful truth of a moral hell which the sinner carried always within him. Lucian would have said, with that great Roman poet who found no refuge from superstition but in materialism,—

"No vultures rend the breast of Tityos,
As his vast bulk lies tost on Acheron's wave ;

. . . . .

But he is Tityos, whose prostrate soul
The fangs of guilty love and vain regret,
And fruitless longings ever vex and tear." *

In that thought, at least, the Christian poet is in accord with the heathen. It is the punishment which Milton imagines for the Great Tempter himself:—

"Horror and doubt distract
His troubled thoughts, and from the bottom stir
The Hell within him ; for within him Hell
He brings, and round about him now from Hell
One step, no more than from himself, can fly
By change of place ; now conscience works despair
That slumbered,—wakes the bitter memory
Of what he was, what is, and what must be." †

* Lucretius, iii. 997. † Par. Lost, iv. 18.

CHARON'S VISIT TO THE UPPER WORLD.

This is one of the author's best pieces, and though classed amongst the miscellaneous Dialogues, may very well find a place here. The *dramatis personæ* are the same, and the contrast between the world of the living and the world of ghosts is still the theme.

MERCURY AND CHARON.

Mercury. What are you laughing about, Charon? And what has made you leave your boat and come up here into our parts? You don't very often favour us with a visit.

Charon. Well, I had a fancy, Master Mercury, to see what kind of a thing human life was, and what men do in the world, and what it is that they have to leave behind them, that they all bemoan themselves so when they come down our way. For you know that never a one of them makes the voyage without tears. So I begged leave of absence from Pluto, just for a day, like Protesilaus, and came up here into the daylight. And I think myself very lucky in falling in with you; you'll be good enough to act as my guide, I know, and go round with me and show me everything —you know all about it.

Merc. Really, Mr Ferryman, I can't spare time. I have to go off to do an errand for Jupiter upon earth. He's very irascible, and if I loiter on the road, I fear he may banish me entirely into your dark dominions, or do to me as he did to Vulcan lately,—take me by the foot and pitch me down from heaven, and so I shall have to go limping round with the wine, like him.

Cha. And will you let me go wandering about the earth and losing my way—you, my old friend and messmate? It wouldn't be amiss for you to remember, my lad, how I have never made you bale the boat, or even pull an oar, but you lie snoring on the deck, for all those great broad shoulders; or if you find any talkative fellow among the dead men, you chatter with him all the way over, leaving a poor old fellow like me to pull both oars myself. By your father's beard, now, my good Mercury, don't go away! Show me round this upper world, that I may see something before I go home again. Why, if you leave me here by myself, I shall be no better than the blind men. Just as they go stumbling about in the darkness, so do I in this confounded light. Oblige me now, Mercury, do—and I'll never forget the favour.

Merc. This job will cost me a beating, I plainly foresee—all the wages I shall get for acting as guide will be blows. But I suppose I must oblige you: what can a fellow do when a friend presses him? But as to seeing everything thoroughly, Mr Ferryman, that's impossible—it would take a matter of years. There would have to be a hue and cry sent after me by Jupiter, as a runaway; and it would stop your business in the service of Death, and Pluto's empire would suffer, by your stopping all transportation there for some time; and then Æacus would be in a rage about his fees, when he found not an obol coming in. But I'll manage to let you see what's best worth seeing.

Cha. You know best, Mercury; I'm a perfect stranger here, and know nought about this upper world.

Merc. First, then, we must find some commanding spot, where you can see everything from. If you could have got up into heaven, now, there would have been no trouble—you might see it all from there, as from a watch-tower. However, since your ghostly functions are a bar to your admittance into Jove's dominions, we must look out for a good high mountain.

Cha. You know what I used to say when we were aboard my boat. Whenever the wind took us on the quarter, and the waves rose high, then you, in your ignorance, would be calling to me to shorten sail, or let go the sheet, or run before the wind,—and I always bid you all sit still and hold your tongues—I knew what was best to be done. So now do you just take what course you think best: you are captain now; and I, as all passengers should do, will sit still and do as you tell me.

Merc. Very right. I know the best plan, and I'll soon find a good look-out place. Would Caucasus do? or is Parnassus higher—or Olympus higher still? When I look at Olympus, a bright idea comes into my head; but you must help me, and do your fair share of the work.

Cha. Give your orders—I'll help as far as I can.

Merc. The poet Homer says that the sons of Aloeus—they were but two, and they were only youths—designed once upon a time to wrench up Ossa and put it on Olympus, and then Pelion on top of that—thinking so to get a good ladder to climb into heaven by. Now those lads suffered for it, and it served them right, for it was a very insolent trick. But you see we are not scheming anything against the gods, so why should not we two roll these mountains one on top of the other, so as to get a good view from a commanding position?

Cha. And could we two by ourselves lift and carry Pelion or Ossa?

Merc. Why not, Charon? you don't mean to say that we are weaker than those two boys,—we, who are divinities?

Cha. No; but the thing itself seems, to my mind, impossible.

Merc. Very likely; because you're so illiterate, Charon, and destitute altogether of the poetic faculty. But that grand Homer makes a road into heaven in two lines—he claps the mountains together so easily. I wonder, too, that this should seem to you such a prodigy, when you know how Atlas bears the weight of the whole globe himself, and carries us all on his back. I suppose you've heard, too, of my brother Hercules, how he supplied Atlas's place once, just to allow him a little rest, while he took the weight upon his own shoulders?

Cha. Yes, I've heard all about it; but whether it be true or not, you and the poet only know.

Merc. Quite true, I assure you, Charon: why should such clever men tell lies? So let's set to work upon Ossa first, as the poet and his verse recommend;

"And on Ossa's top
They rolled the leafy Pelion." *

Do you see how easy it is? We've done it capitally—and most poetically. Now let me get up and see whether it will do, or whether we must build a little higher yet. Ah! we are still under the shadow of Olympus, I see. Only Ionia and Lydia are visible yet on the east: on the west, we can't see further than Italy and Sicily: on the south, only this side the Danube,—and Crete only indistinctly down here. I say, Ferryman, we shall have to move Œta too, and then clap Parnassus on top of all.

Cha. So be it; only take care we don't attempt too much,—I mean, beyond what poetical probability allows. Homer will prove a very unlucky architect for us, if we tumble down with all this weight upon us and break our skulls.

Merc. Never fear—it's all quite safe. Move Œta now—now up with Parnassus. There—now I'll get up and look again. All right—I can see everything. Now you come up too.

Cha. Lend us a hand then, Mercury—it's no joke getting up such a place as this.

Merc. Well, if you want to see everything, you know, Charon, you can't expect to gratify your curiosity and never risk your neck. But take fast hold of my hand—and take care you don't put your foot upon a slippery stone. Well done!—now you're safe up. Parnassus, luckily, has two tops, so you can sit upon

* Hom., Odyss. xi.

one and I on the other. Now look all round you and see what you can see.

Cha. I see a large extent of land, and as it were a great lake all round it, and mountains and rivers bigger than Cocytus or Phlegethon,— and men,— oh! such little creatures! and some kind of hiding-places or burrows they have.

Merc. Those are cities, which you call burrows.

Cha. Do you know, Mercury, we seem to have done no good, after all, in moving Parnassus, and Œta, and these other mountains?

Merc. Why so?

Cha. Because I can see nothing distinctly from this height. I wanted not merely to see cities and hills, as one does in a picture, but men themselves, and what they do, and what they talk about, — as I did when you met me first and found me laughing; I had just been uncommonly amused at something.

Merc. And what was that, pray?

Cha. Some man had been invited by one of his friends to dinner, I conclude, for to-morrow. "I'll be sure to come," says he—and just as he was speaking, down comes a tile from the roof somehow, and kills him. So I laughed to think he couldn't keep his appointment. And now I think I had better get down again, that I may see and hear better.

Merc. Stay where you are. I've a remedy for this difficulty too. I can make you marvellously keen-sighted, by using a certain incantation from Homer, invented for this special purpose. The moment I say the words, you'll find no more difficultv as to vision, but will see everything quite plain.

Cha. Say them, then.

Merc.

"Lo! from this earthly mist I purge thy sight,
That thou may'st know both gods and men aright."*

How now? Can you see better?

Cha. Wonderful! Lynceus himself would be blind in comparison! Now explain things to me, and answer my questions. But first, would you like me to ask you a question out of Homer, that you may see I'm not quite ignorant of the great poet?

Merc. How come you to know anything about him, —a sailor like you, always at the oar?

Cha. Look here now,—that's very disrespectful to my craft. Why, when I carried him across after he was dead, I heard him rhapsodising all the way, and I remember some of it. A terrible storm we had that voyage, too. He began some chant of not very happy omen for seafaring folk,—how Neptune gathered the clouds, and troubled the sea—stirring it up with his trident, like a ladle—rousing all the winds and everything else. He so disturbed the water with his poetry, that all on a sudden we had a perfect tempest about us, and the boat was wellnigh overset. Well, then, he fell sick himself, and vomited up great part of his poem,—Scylla and Charybdis, and the Cyclops, and all. I had no great trouble in picking up a few scraps of the contents. So, as the poet has it,—

* Hom., Il. v. 127.

"Who is yon stalwart warrior, tall and strong,
By head and shoulders towering o'er the throng?"

Merc. That's Milo of Crotona, the great wrestler. The Greeks are applauding him because he has just lifted a bull and is carrying it across the arena.

Cha. They'll have much better reason to applaud me, Mercury, when I get hold of Milo himself, as I shall do very shortly, and clap him on board my boat, when he comes down our way after having been thrown by that invincible wrestler, Death; no back-trick that he knows can manage *him*. He'll weep and groan then, we shall see, when he remembers all his laurels and triumphs; but now he is very proud because they all admire him for carrying the bull. Do you suppose, now, that man ever expects to die?

The visitor from the lower world, under Mercury's instruction, surveys many other scenes in human life. Space and Chronology are, of course, set entirely at defiance under the potent incantation which Mercury has borrowed from the poet — as they are, indeed, sometimes by poets themselves. He sees Cyrus planning his great expedition against Crœsus; overhears the latter monarch holding his celebrated conversation with Solon on the great question of human happiness; is shown the Scythian Tomyris on her white horse, the savage queen who is to give the Persian conqueror "his fill of blood." He sees the too fortunate Polycrates receiving back his lost ring from the fisherman, and learns from his guide (who has heard it as a secret from Clotho) the miserable end of the tyrant's prosperity. Then Mercury shows him the now desolate site of what once was Nineveh, and tells him how the great Babylon is fated to perish in like manner. As for the remains of Mycenæ, and Argos, and, above all, of the renowned Troy,—these Mercury is afraid to show his friend, lest when he returns to the Shades below he should strangle the poet for his exaggerations. The whole dialogue is very fine, and in a higher tone than is Lucian's wont to use, though no writer could use it with better effect.

Cha. Strange and multiform indeed is the crowd I see, and human life seems full of trouble. And their cities are like hives of bees, in which each has his own sting, and therewith attacks his neighbour; and some, like wasps, plunder and harry the weaker. But who are that crowd of shadows, invisible to them, who hover over their heads?

Merc. These, Charon, are Hope, and Fear, and Madness; and Lusts, and Desires, and Passions, and Hate, and suchlike. Of these, Folly mingles with the crowd below, and is, as one may say, their fellow-citizen. So also Hate, and Anger, and Jealousy, and Ignorance, and Distress, and Covetousness. But Fear and Hope hover above them; and the first, when she swoops down upon them, drives them out of their minds, and makes them cower and shudder; whilst Hope, still fluttering over them, the instant one thinks he has surely laid hold of her, flies up out of his reach, and leaves him balked and gaping, like Tantalus below, when the water flies his lips. Also, if you look close, you will see the Fates too hovering over them, each with her spindle, whence are drawn slender threads which are attached to all.

Charon compares human life to the bubbles which rise and float along the stream—some small, which quickly burst and disappear; some larger, which attract others in their course, and so grow larger still, but which soon break also in their turn, and vanish into nothing;* and Mercury assures him that his comparison is quite as good as Homer's celebrated one of the leaves on the trees. It puzzles him also to discover what there is in this life so very desirable, that men should so take the loss of it to heart; and he would fain himself take a journey to earth, and preach wisdom to these miserable mortals, to warn them to "cease from vanity, and live with death ever before their eyes. 'O fools!' I would say to them, 'why are ye anxious about such little things? Cease from thus wearying yourselves; ye cannot live for ever: none of those things ye so admire is everlasting, nor can a man carry aught of it away with him when he dies, but naked he must depart below; and house and lands and gold must change their master, and pass into other hands.'"

But all such preaching, Mercury assures him, would be in vain. Their ears are so fast stopped with error and ignorance, that no surgeon's instrument can bore them. What Lethe does for the dead, obstinacy does

* Jeremy Taylor has adopted and enlarged this passage from Lucian, in the opening paragraph of his "Holy Dying."

for the living. Some there are, however, among these mortals, "whose ears are open to the voice of truth, and whose vision is purged to see the things of human life in their real aspect." Charon would read his lesson, then, to them. "That would be labour lost," replies Mercury, "to teach them what they know well already. See how they sit apart from the vulgar herd, smiling at all that passes, and feeling never any kind of satisfaction in it: but plainly meditating an escape to your quiet regions, out of the weariness of life; hated, moreover, as they are by their fellows, because they seek to convict them of their folly." "These seem but few," says Charon. "They are enough," replies Mercury. Enough to be the salt of the earth; such, even in the heathen's estimate, must always be few. And cynicism and suicide,—these, as we see, were the heathen's remedies for the vanity and vexation of life.

CHAPTER IV.

LUCIAN AND THE PHILOSOPHERS.

THE great success and reputation achieved by the early Greek philosophers, and especially by those who professed Rhetoric and Dialectics, naturally led to the assumption of the character by a host of successors, many of them mere pretenders. It was a profession not only tempting to a man's self-conceit, but to his love of gain: for, in spite of the protest of one at least of the great teachers of antiquity—Socrates—against debasing philosophy to a mere trade by accepting money for discoursing on it, it had not unnaturally become the custom to take fees both for public lectures and for private instruction. For a philosopher had to live, like other men. The Antonine Cæsars, zealous for the education of their subjects, founding lectureships and endowing colleges throughout their empire, possibly encouraged too much the mere pretenders to learning by the liberality of their grants, and the ire of the satirist may have been justly roused by the unworthiness of many of the recipients.*

* "Beaucoup de gens se faisaient philosophes parce que Marc Aurèle les enrichissait."—Champagny, "Les Antonines," iii.

Athens was still the great resort for professors of all sciences, from all countries, and of all characters. The genius of the people insured such visitors a welcome reception. Talk was the Athenian's privilege and his delight. "To tell or to hear some new thing," is St Paul's brief epitome of the life of the Athenian multitude of his day—and contemporary history does but amplify the apostle's report. Nor is it to be supposed that the wisest or the most honest teacher was always the most popular; rather, the boldest and least scrupulous pretenders were perhaps the most sure of an audience. As in our own days, the medicine which is put forward as a cure for all diseases is secure of a wide sale among the vulgar; so the lecturer who professed universal knowledge—and there were plenty of such—did not fail of commending himself to the greedy ears of the Athenian populace. There were men who announced themselves as prepared—for a consideration—to dispute on any imaginable subject of human knowledge, or to reply to any question which curiosity might propose. Especially were those sought after who professed to teach the great secret of beating an opponent in argument, right or wrong; an enviable accomplishment, unfortunately, in the eyes of most intellectual people, but especially of men who took so much part in public life as did the Athenian commons.

To such an extent had this passion for talk in all its forms — whether in propounding the most startling

222. The whole passage, as an illustration of Lucian, well deserves attention.

theories of morals or metaphysics, or in the most ingenious fencing with the weapons of logic and rhetoric —spread itself in Lucian's day, that the abuses of the Schools presented an ample and tempting field for so keen a satirist. Add to this that he himself had been very much as it were behind the scenes; that in so far as he had been a real seeker after wisdom and an honest teacher of the truth, he had seen how these were disregarded by the pretended philosophers of his day; or in so far as he had lent himself to the common temptation, and had regarded gain and reputation more than a conscientious utterance of what truth he knew, he would have experienced how very readily a few specious phrases and plausible assertions pass for wisdom with the multitude, and how often the unintelligible may be made to do duty for the sublime.

Next to the absurdities of the popular religion, then, those of the pretenders to philosophy lay invitingly open to the attack of the satirist. The fact that in both cases such attack had to be made upon a strong position, guarded by much popular prejudice and by many private interests, would be only an additional reason for engaging in it. He looked upon both systems as what a modern satirist would call "enormous shams," and the success of the imposture made the work of unmasking it all the more exciting. In both cases, truth suffered more or less under the undiscriminating ridicule which could not afford to spoil its point by making distinctions and exceptions. As in his merciless dissection of the so-called divinities of the pagan heaven, he seems often to repudiate the existence of any divine principle at all; so when he holds up to derision the charlatans and impostors who sheltered themselves under the names of the great masters of old times, and who pushed their tenets to absurdity, he lays himself open to the charge of caricaturing those venerable sages themselves.

But, in truth, veneration for great names is a luxury in which the satirist by profession can rarely afford to indulge. The exigencies of his craft go nigh to forbid him to hold anything sacred. We know how constantly, even in our more decorous modern days, the man who has a keen taste for humour and a reputation for being amusing is tempted to make jests which savour of profanity, while he may very possibly be no more profane at heart than those who profess themselves shocked by his levity of tone. It has been remarked already, in one of the preceding volumes of this series, in speaking of Aristophanes, that we may be quite wrong in assuming that he bore any malice against Socrates, or was insensible to the higher qualities of his character, because he found that it suited his purpose to caricature some of the eccentricities of so well known a personage for the comic stage: and we may be doing Lucian equal injustice in accusing him of atheism, because in his writings he touches only the absurd side of a faith which was fast passing away and leaving as yet nothing in its place; or in thinking that he sneers at all great intellectual discoveries, because he found in the contradictions and the sophistries of the Schools such congenial matter for his pen. And although, like Aristophanes, he uses well-known names from time to time for the persons of his drama, anything like what we call personality was probably far from his thoughts. "Lucian," says Ranke, "spoke after the manner of ancient comedy,—things true, not of this or that individual, but of bodies, of communities, of society in general."

With this reservation the reader will perhaps judge more fairly the broad farce—for this is what it really is—of the Dialogue which follows.

THE SALE OF THE PHILOSOPHERS.

Scene, a Slave-mart; JUPITER, MERCURY, PHILOSOPHERS *in the garb of slaves for sale; audience of Buyers.*

Jupiter. Now, you arrange the benches, and get the place ready for the company. You bring out the goods, and set them in a row; but trim them up a little first, and make them look their best, to attract as many customers as possible. You, Mercury, must put up the lots, and bid all comers welcome to the sale.—Gentlemen, we are here going to offer you philosophical systems of all kinds, and of the most varied and ingenious description. If any gentleman happens to be short of ready money, he can give his security for the amount, and pay next year.

Mercury (to Jupiter). There are a great many come; so we had best begin at once, and not keep them waiting.

Jup. Begin the sale, then.

Merc. Whom shall we put up first?

Jup. This fellow with the long hair,—the Ionian. He's rather an imposing personage.

Merc. You, Pythagoras! step out, and show yourself to the company.

Jup. Put him up.

Merc. Gentlemen, we here offer you a professor of the very best and most select description—who buys? Who wants to be a cut above the rest of the world? Who wants to understand the harmonies of the universe? and to live two lives? *

Customer (*turning the Philosopher round and examining him*). He's not bad to look at. What does he know best?

* Mr Grote, in the introductory chapter of his Plato, thus sketches the Pythagorean doctrine of "The Music of the Spheres." "The revolutions of such grand bodies [the Sun and Planets] could not take place, in the opinion of the Pythagoreans, without producing a loud and powerful sound; and as their distances from the central fire were supposed to be arranged in musical ratios, so the result of all these separate sounds was full and perfect harmony. To the objection—Why were not these sounds heard by us?—they replied, that we had heard them constantly and without intermission from the hour of our birth; hence they had become imperceptible by habit."

The "two lives" is of course an allusion to Pythagoras's notion of the transmigration of souls. It is said of him that he professed to be conscious of having been formerly Euphorbus, one of the chiefs present at the siege of Troy, and of having subsequently borne other shapes. There is also a story of his having interfered on behalf of a dog which was being beaten, declaring that in its cries he recognised "the voice of a departed friend."

Merc. Arithmetic, astronomy, prognostics, geometry, music, and conjuring—you've a first-rate soothsayer before you.

Cust. May one ask him a few questions?

Merc. Certainly—(*aside*) and much good may the answers do you.

Cust. What country do you come from?

Pythagoras. Samos.

Cust. Where were you educated?

Pyth. In Egypt, among the wise men there.

Cust. Suppose I buy you, now—what will you teach me?

Pyth. I will teach you nothing—only recall things to your memory.*

Cust. How will you do that?

Pyth. First, I will clean out your mind, and wash out all the rubbish.

Cust. Well, suppose that done, how do you proceed to refresh the memory?

Pyth. First, by long repose, and silence—speaking no word for five whole years.†

* That "all knowledge is but recollection" is an assertion attributed both to Pythagoras and Plato. The idea of "an immortal soul always learning and forgetting in successive periods of existence, having seen and known all things at one time or other, and by association with one thing capable of recovering all," may be seen discussed in Plato's Dialogue, "Meno," 81, 82, &c.

† The injunction of a period of silence upon neophytes (the "five years" is most likely an exaggeration) was plainly meant as a check upon their presuming to teach before they had matured their knowledge. "It would be not unserviceable" (says Tooke) "in our own age, by preventing many of our raw

Cust. Why, look ye, my good fellow, you'd best go teach the dumb son of Crœsus! I want to talk, and not be a dummy. Well,—but after this silence and these five years?

Pyth. You shall learn music and geometry.

Cust. A queer idea, that one must be a fiddler before one can be a wise man!

Pyth. Then you shall learn the science of numbers.

Cust. Thank you, but I know how to count already.

Pyth. How do you count?

Cust. One, two, three, four—

Pyth. Ha! what you call four is ten, and the perfect triangle, and the great oath by which we swear.*

Cust. Now, so help me the great Ten and Four, I never heard more divine or more wonderful words!

Pyth. And afterwards, stranger, you shall learn about Earth, and Air, and Water, and Fire,—what is their action, and what their form, and what their motion.

Cust. What! have Fire, Air, or Water bodily shape?

Pyth. Surely they have; else, without form and shape, how could they move?—Besides, you shall learn that the Deity consists in Number, Mind, and Harmony.

Cust. What you say is really wonderful!

Pyth. Besides what I have just told you, you shall

young divines exposing themselves in the pulpit before they have read their Greek Testament."

* Ten being the sum of 1, 2, 3, 4. Number, in the system of Pythagoras, was the fundamental principle of all things: in the Monad—Unity—he recognised the Deity.

understand that you yourself, who seem to be one individual, are really somebody else.

Cust. What! do you mean to say I'm somebody else, and not myself, now talking to you?

Pyth. Just at this moment you are; but once upon a time you appeared in another body, and under another name; and hereafter you will pass again into another shape still.

[After a little more discussion of this philosopher's tenets, he is purchased on behalf of a company of professors from Magna Grecia, for ten minæ. The next lot is Diogenes, the Cynic.]

Merc. Who'll you have next? That dirty fellow from Pontus?

Jup. Ay—he'll do.

Merc. Here! you with the wallet on your back,—you round-shouldered fellow! come out, and walk round the ring.—A grand character, here, gentlemen; a most extraordinary and remarkable character, I may say; a really free man here I have to offer you—who'll buy?

Cust. How say you, Mr Salesman? Sell a free citizen?

Merc. Oh yes.

Cust. Are you not afraid he may bring you before the court of Areopagus for kidnapping?

Merc. Oh, he doesn't mind about being sold; he says he's free wherever he goes or whatever becomes of him.

Cust. But what could one do with such a dirty,

wretched-looking body — unless one were to make a ditcher or a water-carrier of him?

Merc. Well, or if you employ him as door-porter, you'll find him more trustworthy than any dog. In fact, 'Dog' is his name.

Cust. Where does he come from, and what does he profess?

Merc. Ask him—that will be most satisfactory.

Cust. I'm afraid of him, he looks so savage and sulky; perhaps he'll bark if I go near him, or even bite me, I shouldn't wonder. Don't you see how he handles his club, and knits his brows, and looks threatening and angry?

Merc. Oh, there's no fear—he's quite tame.

Cust. (*approaching Diogenes cautiously*). First, my good fellow, of what country are you?

Diogenes (*surlily*). All countries.

Cust. How can that be?

Diog. I'm a citizen of the world.

Cust. What master do you profess to follow?

Diog. Hercules.

Cust. Why don't you adopt the lion's hide, then? I see you have the club.

Diog. Here's my lion's hide,—this old cloak. Like Hercules, I wage war against pleasure; but not under orders, as he did, but of my own free will. My choice is to cleanse human life.

Cust. A very good choice too. But what do you profess to know best? or of what art are you master?

Diog. I am the liberator of mankind, the physician

of the passions; in short, I claim to be the prophet of truth and liberty.

Cust. Come now, Sir Prophet, suppose I buy you, after what fashion will you instruct me?

Diog. I shall first take and strip you of all your luxury, confine you to poverty, and put an old garment on you: then I shall make you work hard, and lie on the ground, and drink water only, and fill your belly with whatever comes first; your money, if you have any, at my bidding you must take and throw into the sea; and you must care for neither wife nor children, nor country; and hold all things vanity; and leave your father's house and sleep in an empty tomb, or a ruined tower,—ay, or in a tub: and have your wallet filled with lentils, and parchments close-written on both sides. And in this state you shall profess yourself happier than the King of the East. And if any man beats you, or tortures you, this you shall hold to be not painful at all.

Cust. How! do you mean to say I shall not feel pain when I'm beaten? Do you think I've the shell of a crab or a tortoise, man?

Diog. You can quote that line of Euripides, you know,—slightly altered.

Cust. And what's that, pray?

Diog.

"Thy mind shall feel pain, but thy tongue confess none." *

But the qualifications you will most require are these: you must be unscrupulous, and brazen-faced, and ready

* This unfortunate quibble of Euripides, which he puts into

to revile prince and peasant alike; so shall men take notice of you, and hold you for a brave man. Moreover, let your speech be rough, and your voice harsh, and in fact like a dog's growl; and your countenance rigid, and your gait corresponding to it, and your manner generally brute-like and savage. All modesty and gentleness and moderation put far from you; the faculty of blushing you must eradicate utterly. Seek the most crowded haunts of men; but when there, keep solitary, and hold converse with none; address neither friend nor stranger, for that would be the ruin of your empire. Do in sight of all what others are almost ashamed to do alone. At the last, if you choose, choke yourself with a raw polypus, or an onion.* And this happy consummation I devoutly wish you.

Cust. (*recovering from some astonishment*). Get out with you! what abominable and unnatural principles!

Diog. But very easy to carry out, mind you, and not at all difficult to learn. One needs no education, or reading, or such nonsense, for this system; it's the real short cut to reputation. Be you the most ordinary person,—cobbler, sausagemonger, carpenter, pawn-

the mouth of Hippolytus in his play (Hipp. 612) as a defence of perjury,—

"My tongue hath sworn it—but my thought was free"—

was a never-failing subject of parody to his critics and satirists.

* The first mode of suicide was said to have been adopted by the philosopher Democritus.

broker, — nothing hinders your being the object of popular admiration, provided only that you've impudence enough, and brass enough, and a happy talent for bad language.

Cust. Well, I don't require your instructions in that line. Possibly, however, you might do for a bargeman or a gardener,* at a pinch, if this party has a mind to sell you for a couple of oboli,— I couldn't give more.

Merc. (*eagerly*). Take him at your own bidding; we're glad to get rid of him, he is so troublesome, — bawls so, and insults everybody up and down, and uses such very bad language.

Jup. Call out the next—the Cyrenaic there, in purple, with the garland on.

Merc. Now, gentlemen, let me beg your best attention. This next lot is a very valuable one — quite suited to parties in a good position. Here's Pleasure and Perfect Happiness, all for sale! Who'll give me a bidding now, for perpetual luxury and enjoyment? [*A Cyrenaic, bearing traces of recent debauch, staggers into the ring.*]

Cust. Come forward here, and tell us what you know: I shouldn't mind buying you, if you've any useful qualities.

Merc. Don't disturb him, sir, if you please, just now—don't ask him any questions. The truth is, he

* For the accomplishments of the bargemen and vine-dressers in the way of bad language we have Horace's testimony, Sat. i. 5 and 7. The first-mentioned fraternity bear the same reputation still.

has taken a little too much; that's why he doesn't answer—his tongue's not quite steady.

Cust. And who in their senses, do you suppose, would buy such a debauched and drunken rascal? Faugh! how he stinks of unguents! and look how he staggers and goes from side to side as he walks!* But tell us, now, Mercury, what qualifications he really has, and what he knows anything about.

Merc. Well, he's very pleasant company—good to drink with, and can sing and dance a little—useful to a master who is a man of pleasure and fond of a gay life. Besides, he is a good cook, and clever in made dishes—and, in short, a complete master of the science of luxury. He was brought up at Athens, and was once in the service of the Tyrants of Sicily, who gave him a very good character. The sum of his principles is to despise everything, to make use of everything, and to extract the greatest amount of pleasure from everything.

Cust. Then you must look out for some other purchaser, among the rich and wealthy here; I can't afford to buy such an expensive indulgence.

Merc. I fear, Jupiter, we shall have this lot left on our hands—he's unsaleable.

* If this be really meant for Aristippus, the founder of the Cyrenaic philosophy, it is the most unfair presentation of all. However some of his followers might have abused his principles, his own character is probably much more fairly described by Horace:—

> "All lives sat well on Aristippus; though
> He liked the high, he yet could grace the low."
> —Ep. I. xvii.

Jup. Put him aside, and bring out another. Stay, —those two there, that fellow from Abdera who is always laughing, and the Ephesian, who is always crying; I've a mind to sell them as a pair.

Merc. Stand out there in the ring, you two.—We offer you here, sirs, two most admirable characters, the wisest we've had for sale yet.

Cust. By Jove, they're a remarkable contrast! Why, one of them never stops laughing, while the other seems to be in trouble about something, for he's in tears all the time. Holloa, you fellow! what's all this about? What are you laughing at?

Democritus. Need you ask? Because everything seems to me so ridiculous—you yourselves included.

Cust. What! do you mean to laugh at us all to our faces, and mock at all we say and do?

Dem. Undoubtedly; there's nothing in life that's serious. Everything is unreal and empty—a mere fortuitous concurrence of indefinite atoms.

Cust. You're an indefinite atom yourself, you rascal! Confound your insolence, won't you stop laughing? But you there, poor soul (*to Heraclitus*), why do you weep so? for there seems more use in talking to you.

Heraclitus. Because, stranger, everything in life seems to me to call for pity and to deserve tears; there is nothing but what is liable to calamity; wherefore I mourn for men, and pity them. The evil of to-day I regard not much: but I mourn for that which is to come hereafter—the burning and destruction of all things. This I grieve for, and that nothing is permanent, but all mingled, as it were, in one bitter cup,

—pleasure that is no pleasure, knowledge that knows nothing, greatness that is so little, all going round and round and taking their turn in this game of life.

Cust. What do you hold human life to be, then?

Her. A child at play, handling its toys, and changing them with every caprice.

Cust. And what are men?

Her. Gods—but mortal.

Cust. And the gods?

Her. Men—but immortal.

Cust. You speak in riddles, fellow, and put us off with puzzles. You are as bad as Apollo Loxias, giving oracles that no man can understand.

Her. Yea; I trouble not myself for any of ye.

Cust. Then no man in his senses is like to buy you.

Her. Woe! woe to every man of ye, I say! buyers or not buyers.

Cust. Why, this fellow is pretty near mad!—I'll have nought to do with either of them, for my part.

Merc. (*turning to Jupiter*). We shall have this pair left on our hands too.

Jup. Put up another.

Merc. Will you have that Athenian there, who talks so much?

Jup. Ay—try him.

Merc. Step out, there!—A highly moral character, gentlemen, and very sensible. Who makes me an offer for this truly pious lot?

[The morality which the satirist puts into the mouth of Socrates, in his replies to the interrogatories of his would-be purchaser, is that which was attributed to him —probably quite without foundation—by his enemies. The customer next asks, where he lives?]

Socrates. I live in a certain city of mine own building, a new model Republic, and I make laws for myself.*

Cust. I should like to hear one of them.

Soc. Listen to my grand law of all, then, about wives—that no man should have a wife of his own, but that all should have wives in common.

Cust. What! do you mean to say you have abrogated all the laws of marriage?

Soc. It puts an end, you see, to so many difficult questions, and so much litigation in the divorce courts.

Cust. Grand idea that! But what is the main feature of your philosophy?

Soc. The existence of ideals and patterns of all things in nature. Everything you see—the earth, and all that is on it, the heavens, the sea—of all these there exist invisible ideals, external to this visible universe.

Cust. And pray where are they?

Soc. Nowhere. If they were confined to any place, you see, they could not be at all.

Cust. I never see any of these ideals of yours.

Soc. Of course not: the eyes of your soul are blind. But I can see the ideals of all things. I see

* It must be remembered that Plato, in his 'Republic,' makes Socrates the expositor of his new polity throughout; he had probably derived at least the leading ideas from him.

an invisible double of yourself, and another self besides myself—in fact, I see everything double.

Cust. Bless me! I must buy you, you are so very clever and sharp-sighted. Come (*turning to Mercury*), what do you ask for him?

Merc. Give us two talents for him.

Cust. I'll take him at your price. I'll pay you another time.

Merc. What's your name?

Cust. Dion, of Syracuse.

Merc. (*makes a note*). Take him, and good luck to you. Now, Epicurus, we want you. Who'll buy this lot? He's a disciple of that laughing fellow, and also of the other drunken party, whom we put up just now. He knows more than either of them, however, on one point—he's more of an infidel. Otherwise, he's a pleasant fellow, and fond of good eating.

Cust. What's his price?

Merc. Two minæ.

Cust. Here's the money. But just tell us what he likes best.

Merc. Oh, anything sweet—honey-cakes, and figs especially.

Cust. They're easily got; Carian figs are cheap enough.

Jup. Now then, call another—him with the shaven crown there, and gloomy looks—the one we got from the Porch yonder.

Merc. You're right. I fancy a good many of our customers who have come to the sale are waiting to bid for him.—Now I'm going to offer you the most perfect article of all—Virtue personified. Who wants to be the only man who knows everything?

Cust. What do you mean?

Merc. I mean that here you have the only wise man, the only handsome man, the only righteous man, the true and only king, general, orator, legislator, and everything else there is.*

Cust. The true and only cook then, I conclude, and cobbler, and carpenter, and so forth?

Merc. I conclude so too.

Cust. Come then, my good fellow—if I'm to purchase you, tell me all about yourself; and first let me ask, with all these wonderful qualifications, are you not mortified at being put up for sale here as a slave?

Chrysippus. Not at all: such things are external to ourselves, and whatever is external to ourselves, it follows must be matters of indifference to us.

[The Stoic proceeds to explain his tenets, in the technical jargon of his school—which his listener declares to be utterly incomprehensible, and on which modern readers would pronounce much the same judg-

* Lucian had evidently in his mind the humorous sketch of the Stoic given by Horace, Sat. i. 3 :—

> "What though the wise ne'er shoe or slipper made,
> The wise is still a brother of the trade,—
> Just as Hermogenes, when silent, still
> Remains a singer of consummate skill—
> As sly Alfenius, when he had let drop
> His implements of art and shut up shop,
> Was still a barber,—so the wise is best
> In every craft, a king's among the rest."—(Conington.)

ment. His great accomplishment lies, as he himself professes, in the skilful handling of sophisms—"word-nets," as he calls them—in which he entangles his opponents, stops their mouths, and reduces them to silence. He gives an example of his art, which is a curious specimen of the kind of folly to which the wisdom of the ancients occasionally condescended. A crocodile is supposed to have seized a boy in crossing a river, and promises to restore him to his father if this latter can guess correctly what he intends to do with him. If he guesses that the crocodile means to give him back, he has guessed wrong, because the crocodile's real intention is to eat him. If he guesses that the crocodile means to eat him, why then, if the crocodile gives him back after all, the guess would plainly be proved wrong by the result; so that there seems no chance for the father, guess which he will. The philosopher assures his listener that this is but one out of many choice examples of the sophistical art with which he is prepared to furnish him; and when the other retorts upon him somewhat in his own style, the Stoic threatens to knock him down with an "indemonstrable syllogism," the effect of which, he warns him, will be to plunge him into "eternal doubt, everlasting silence, and distraction of mind." In the end, however, he is purchased by his interrogator for "self and company." The next who is put up for sale is "the Peripatetic," by whom Aristotle is clearly intended. With him the satirist deals briefly and lightly, as though he had some tenderness for that particular school. "You will find him," says the auctioneer, "moderate, upright, consistent in his life—and what makes him yet more valuable is that in him you are really buying *two* men." "How do you make that out?" asks the customer. "Because," explains Mercury, "he appears to be one person outside and another inside; and remember, if you buy him, you must call one '*esoteric*' and the other '*exoteric.*'" With such recommendations, the Peripatetic finds a ready purchaser for the large sum of twenty minæ. Last comes the Sceptic, Pyrrho, who figures, by a slight change of name, as Pyrrhia, a common appellation for a barbarian slave. The intending purchaser asks him a few questions.]

Cust. Tell me, now, what do you know?

Pyrrhia. Nothing.

Cust. What do you mean?

Pyrrh. That nothing seems to me certain.

Cust. Are we ourselves nothing?

Pyrrh. Well, that is what I am not sure of.

Cust. Don't you know whether you are anything yourself?

Pyrrh. That is what I am still more in doubt about.

Cust. What a creature of doubts it is! And what are those scales for, pray?

Pyrrh. I weigh arguments in them, and balance them one against another; and then, when I find them precisely equal and of the same weight, why, I find it impossible to tell which of them is true.

Cust. Well, is there anything you can do in any other line of business?

Pyrrh. Anything, except catch a runaway slave.

Cust. And why can't you do that?

Pyrrh. Because, you see, I've no faculty of *apprehension.**

Cust. So I should think—you seem to me quite slow and stupid. And now, what do you consider the main end of knowledge?

Pyrrh. Ignorance—to hear nothing and see nothing.

Cust. You confess yourself blind and deaf then?

Pyrrh. Yea, and void of sense and perception, and in no wise differing from a worm.

Cust. I must buy you. (*To Mercury.*) What shall we say for him?

Merc. An Attic mina.

Cust. Here 'tis. Now, fellow, have I bought you or not—tell me?

Pyrrh. Well, it's a doubtful question.

Cust. Not at all—at least I've paid for you.

Pyrrh. I reserve my opinion on that point; it requires consideration.

Cust. Follow me, at all events—that's a servant's duty.

Pyrrh. Are you sure you're stating a fact?

Cust. (*impatiently*). There's the auctioneer, and there's the money, and there are the bystanders to witness.

Pyrrh. Are you sure there are any bystanders?

* The pun here happens to be the same in English as in Greek. But the Athenians were fonder of such word-play than we are.

Cust. I'll have you off to the grinding-house,* sir, and make you feel I'm your master by very tangible proofs.

Pyrrh. Stay—I should like to argue that point a little.

[The doubting philosopher is hurried off, still unconvinced, by Mercury and his new owner, and the sale is adjourned to the next day, when Mercury promises the public that he shall have some cheaper bargains to offer. The whole scene reads like a passage from the old Aristophanic comedy; and though some of the allusions must necessarily lose much of their pungency from our comparative ignorance of the popular philosophy of Lucian's day, the humour of it is still sufficiently entertaining.]

The professors of the various Schools of Philosophy may well be supposed to have been loud in their indignation at this caricature, and in their denunciation of the author. Or at least it suited Lucian's purpose to assume that they were so, and to make the wrath of the solemn fraternity, real or imagined, the subject of a Dialogue which follows by way of sequel to the first. Possibly, also, he desired to guard against any misconception of his purpose in the satire, and to make it clear that it was not against true philosophy or sound science that he directed his wit, but against shallow and conceited pretenders. This second Dialogue—"The Resuscitated Professors"—presents the author flying for his life, pursued by a body of irate philosophers of all sects,

* Slaves who misbehaved were sent there, as the hardest work.

who have obtained one day's leave of absence from the Shades below to avenge themselves on their libeller.

THE RESUSCITATED PROFESSORS.

Socrates. Pelt the wretch! pelt him with volleys of stones,—throw clods at him,—oyster-shells! Beat the blasphemer with your clubs—don't let him escape! Hit him, Plato! and you, Chrysippus! and you!—Form a phalanx, and rush on him all together! As Homer says—"Let wallet join with wallet, club with club!" He is the common enemy of us all, and there is no man among ye whom he has not insulted. You, Diogenes, now use that staff of yours, if ever you did! Don't stop! let him have it, blasphemer that he is! What! tired already, Epicurus and Aristippus? You ought not to be:—

"Be men, professors! summon all your pluck!"

Aristotle, do run a little faster!—That's good! we've caught the beast! We've got you, you rascal! You shall soon find out who you've been abusing! Now what shall we do with him? Let us think of some multiform kind of death, that may suffice for all of us—for he deserves a separate death from each.

Philosopher A. I vote that he be impaled.

Phil. B. Yes—but be well scourged first.

Phil. C. Let his eyes be gouged out.

Phil. D. Ay—but his tongue should be cut out first.

Soc. What think you, Empedocles?

Empedocles. He should be thrown down the crater

of some volcano, and so learn not to revile his betters.

Plato. Nay—the best punishment for him will be that, like Pentheus or Orpheus,—

> "Torn by the ragged rocks he meet his fate."

Lucian. Oh no, no, pray! spare me, for the love of heaven!

Soc. Sentence is passed: nothing can save you. For, as Homer says,—

> "'Twixt men and lions, say, what truce can hold?"

Luc. And I implore you, too, in Homer's words—you will respect him, perhaps, and not reject me, when I give you a recitation,—

> "Spare a brave foe, and take a ransom meet,
> Good bronze, and gold—which even wise men love." *

But his captors have an answer ready out of Homer's inexhaustible repertory; and an appeal which the prisoner makes to Euripides is met in a similar manner. Lucian begs at least to be heard in his own defence. He will prove that he is really the champion and patron of true philosophy, to whom he owes all that he knows. Let him at least have a fair trial, before any judge they please. None can be better than Philosophy herself; but where can she be found? Lucian himself does not know where she lives, though he has often made inquiry. He has seen men in grave

* Parodied from Homer, Il. x. 378, &c. But the last half-line is Lucian's own.

habits, with long beards, who *ought* to have known, but they have always misdirected him. He has seen, too, a flaunting woman, affecting to represent her, whose hall of audience was thronged with visitors; but he had soon detected her as a mere impostor.

Plato agrees with him, that the dwelling of Philosophy is hard to find, nor is her door open to all idle comers. But while they are speaking, they meet her walking in the portico; and to her, by consent of both parties, the prisoner's case is referred. Virtue, and Temperance, and Justice, and Education, who are walking in her company, shall be her assessors in the court; and Truth, "a colourless form, all but imperceptible" —of whom Lucian himself has but a dim glimpse— who brings with her Liberty and Free-speech. The court is held in the temple of Minerva. The aggrieved parties have to choose one of their number as formal accuser; and Chrysippus, in words of high eulogy which may fairly be taken to express the serious opinion of the author himself, suggests Plato as the fittest for that office. The "marvellous sublimity of thought, the Attic sweetness of diction, the persuasive grace, and sagacity, and accuracy, and apposite illustrations; the delicate irony and rapid interrogation," which are here attributed to the great philosopher, are all too genuine characteristics to have been introduced ironically. But Plato declines the office, and the Cynic Diogenes undertakes it, readily enough, disgusted as he is at having been valued at no more than two oboli at the late "Sale." He accuses Lucian of endeavouring to bring all philosophy into contempt.

He is worse than the comedy-writers, Eupolis and Aristophanes, who could at least plead in their excuse the recognised licence of the Dionysiac festivals. He calls for such a sentence on this profane libeller as may deter others from following his example. Lucian defends himself by protesting that it is only sham philosophers, "asses in lions' skins," who shelter their pretensions under the shadow of great names, that he has attacked; it is they, not he, who bring Philosophy into contempt. Such gross misrepresentations as theirs are the less excusable because of the dignity of the things which they misrepresent. "The actor who performs badly the part of a slave or a messenger is guilty of but a venial fault; but to present a Jupiter or a Hercules to the audience in a fashion unworthy of the dignity of the character becomes wellnigh a profanation."

The satirist is triumphantly acquitted. Even Plato and Diogenes withdrew their accusation, and join in hailing him as the real friend of Truth. It is resolved to call up the false pretenders to philosophy for trial before the same court. Lucian desires "Syllogism"—that useful instrument of argument, who acts as crier of the court—to summon them for this purpose; but a strict logical examination is exactly what these professors shrink from. Lucian succeeds, however, in securing their attendance by a proclamation of his own. He announces a public distribution of money and corn in the Acropolis; and whoever can show a very long beard shall be entitled to a basket of figs into the bargain. They come in crowds—Stoics, Peripatetics, and Epicureans, each claiming to be served first. But as soon as they hear of the investigation into their lives and morals, as well as their professions, which is to take place, all but two or three take to flight in a panic. Then Lucian adopts another plan to catch them for examination: he hangs out from the wall of the Acropolis a fisherman's rod and line, baited with a cluster of figs and a purse of gold. They take the bait eagerly, and are hauled up one after another; and as each of the masters of philosophy repudiates all knowledge of them as true disciples, are thrown headlong from the rock. But as there is a risk lest some strong fish should break the line and make off with the bait, Lucian goes down into the city accompanied by Conviction (one of Philosophy's suite), prepared under her guidance to crown with olive such as can stand the test, and to brand conspicuously on the forehead, with the impression of a fox or an ape, all whose profession is a mere cloak for selfish ends. He foretells that they will require for their purpose very few olive crowns, but a good supply of branding-irons.

THE BANQUET; OR, THE MODERN BATTLE OF THE LAPITHÆ.

This is another humorous attack upon the Schools of Philosophy in general, cast in the form of a dialogue. There has been a wedding supper-party at the house of an Athenian of some rank, on the occasion of the marriage of his son, of which Lycinus (*i.e.*, Lucian) here gives an account in a conversation with a friend. He apologises—ironically—for telling the story at all;

he protests against betraying the secrets of hospitality; he declares that, like the poet, he "hates a guest who has a retentive memory;" but since the tale has already, he finds, got abroad,—why, perhaps he had better tell it himself, in order that at least it may be told truly. His friend is sure that in point of fact he is burning to tell it, and threatens, if he affects any more scruple in the matter, to go to some one else for his information.

Then Lucian begins his narrative. There had been invited to this banquet representatives of all the different schools,—Stoic, Peripatetic, and Epicurean, and a "grammarian" (what we should call a "literary man") and a rhetorician besides. Io the Platonist, known in the circles of schoolmen as "The Model," tutor to the young bridegroom, also enters among the guests, and is treated by the host and by most of the company with great consideration and respect, though the Stoic insisted upon being assigned the highest seat. Alcidamas, the Cynic, came in last, without an invitation, quoting, as an impudent sort of apology, the words of Homer—

> "But Menelaus uninvited came."

To which one of the guests whispered a very apposite reply from the same poet—

> "Howbeit this pleased not Agamemnon's heart."

The good host, however, though all the seats were already filled, with much courtesy offered him a stool; but this the Cynic declined as an effeminate and needless luxury. He preferred, he said, to take his food standing; and accordingly ate his supper, as Lucian describes it, "in a kind of nomad fashion, like the Scythians, looking out the best pastures, and following the dishes as the slaves handed them round." And still, as he ate and drank, he declaimed loudly against the luxury of such entertainments, until the host stopped his mouth with a cup of strong wine. The Peripatetic philosopher was observed to be flirting surreptitiously with a pretty waiting-maid,—a proceeding to which the host had to put a stop by sending her quietly out of the room, and substituting a rough-looking groom in her place. As the wine went round, and tongues were loosened, the rhetorician began to recite passages from his orations; while the *littérateur*, not content with quoting Pindar and Anacreon, went on to favour the company with a very tiresome extempore poem of his own. There was a hired jester present, who, of course, launched his jokes indiscriminately, as occasion offered, at all the company. Most of them took it good-humouredly enough; but the Cynic, accustomed to make jests instead of being the subject of them, lost his temper, and engaged in a match at fisticuffs with the poor buffoon, who was a mere pigmy of a man, but who nevertheless gave him a good thrashing, to the great delight of the company.

But at this stage of the entertainment a slave entered with a note. One Stoic professor had been left out of the list of invitations, and had sent an angry remonstrance, in the form of a kind of speech, which the slave was instructed to read. "Though, as was well known, he disliked and despised feasts, as a mere form of sensual gratification; still, ingratitude was a thing he could *not* bear. Forgotten? accidentally overlooked? Oh no, —that excuse would not do. Twice that very morning he had purposely made his bow to his friend Aristænetus. No one can be expected to put up with such marked neglect. Even Diana could not forgive not having been invited to the sacrifice of Œneus. He begs to enclose a philosophical problem which he challenges the whole party of these pretenders who have been preferred to him to solve if they can. He could tell a story about the bridegroom, too, but—never mind. And he begs to say in conclusion, that it is no use to think of appeasing his righteous indignation by offering now to send a present of game, or anything of that kind, by his servant,—the man has strict orders not to take it."

Lucian declares he was quite ashamed when he heard this production read. "You could never have expected such mean and unworthy language," he says, "from a man of his hoary hairs and grave demeanour." The Peripatetic philosopher took occasion from it at once to attack the Stoics generally in the most unmeasured language. One of that school who was in the company retaliated in similar terms—all the professors set to work to abuse each other, and ended by throwing wine in each other's faces, and indulging in other social courtesies of a like kind.

"I could not help reflecting," says the satirist, "how little the learning of the Schools avails us, if it does nothing to improve and dignify the intercourse of daily life. Here were scholars of the highest mark making themselves worse than ridiculous in the eyes of the company! Can it be true that, as some say, much poring over books, and stuffing their heads with other people's ideas, makes men lose their common-sense? Such conduct cannot in this case be laid to the charge of the wine,—for the letter-writer at least was sober. Yet here are the unlearned portion of the company behaving themselves quietly and modestly, while such is the example set them by these professors of wisdom!"

Io, the Platonist, now tried to quiet the uproar by proposing a subject for discussion, upon which, after the fashion of the Dialogues of Plato, each should be allowed to speak in his turn and without interruption. He suggested "Marriage" as an appropriate theme, and proceeded to deliver his own opinion thereupon, which is, of course, that of his great master, as broached in his 'Republic,' and as we have had it set forth by Socrates in his examination at the "Sale." * It would be far better if men would make up their minds to do without it altogether; but as this seems improbable, at least he would recommend the abolition of the prejudice in favour of having separate wives. Lucian thought this expression of opinion somewhat curious, to say the very least, upon such an occasion. The literary gentleman, instead of giving his own views on the question, took the opportunity of reciting to the company an epithalamium of his own composition, which is no doubt a fair burlesque of the common style of such productions. Then, as it grew late, the guests began to make their

* See p. 104.

preparations for departure; and each proceeded to pack up and carry home, as was the custom at such entertainments, some little delicacy set apart for them by their liberal host. They quarrelled again, however, in their greediness, over the largest portions and the fattest fowls. A "free fight" of philosophers ensued, which Lucian could only aptly compare with the battle between the Centaurs and Lapithæ at the marriage of Pirithous. In the midst of it Alcidamas the Cynic, by design or accident, upset the lamp, and the combatants were left for a while in darkness. When it was suddenly relighted, some awkward revelations were made. The Peripatetic moralist was discovered making fierce love to a music-girl, while the Epicurean was concealing under his robe a gold cup which he had snatched from the table. Wounded and bleeding, the combatants were assisted from the room by their attendant slaves. But even thus they could not resist a gibe or two at parting. The Epicurean, with two teeth knocked out in the scuffle, saw the Stoic professor with a damaged eye and his nose bleeding, and bids him remember that, according to his own tenets, "Pain is no real evil." Lucian could only sum up the moral, he tells his friend, in the words of Euripides,—

"How strange and various are the fates of men!
The gods still bring to pass the unforeseen,
And what we look for never comes at all." *

For what could possibly be more unexpected than

* The somewhat weak "tag" common to several of Euripides's plays.

such a termination to a philosophical and literary symposium?

HERMOTIMUS.

This Dialogue, between the author himself as Lycinus and a disciple of the Stoic school, though rather of graver cast than either of the preceding, has yet a great deal of quiet humour in it, and bears token of careful finish. It is a good-humoured blow at the Stoics, and through them at the theories of philosophers generally: but it seems to convey also a graver lesson, which was probably often present to a mind like Lucian's,—that wisdom is hard to find, and that human life is not long enough for the successful pursuit of her.

Lycinus meets Hermotimus going to one of his master's lectures. The student walks with a meditative air, repeating mentally his lesson of yesterday: for, as he explains, he must lose no time; "life is short, and art is long," as said the great Hippocrates; and if it were true of physic, still more true is it of philosophy. Lycinus remarks that as, to his certain knowledge, Hermotimus has been studying hard for the last twenty years, much to the detriment of his health and his complexion, he should have conceived that he must by this time be very near the attainment of the goal of happiness—if that be synonymous with wisdom. "Nay," replies the other; "Virtue, as Hesiod tells us, dwells afar off, and the road to her is long, and very steep and rough, and costs no small toil to them that travel it." He himself is as yet only at the foot of the mountain. And when does he hope to get to the top? Well, Hermotimus thinks possibly in another twenty years or so. Lycinus remarks that a man might go three times round the world in that time: and can his master promise him that he will live so long? He hopes so, at least; and one day—one minute—of enjoyment on the summit, if once attained, will recompense him fully for all his time and pains. But is he sure again that the happiness he seeks there, and of which he can have as yet no kind of experience, will be found worth the search? and in what is it to consist? glory, riches, exquisite pleasures—is that what he expects? Hermotimus bids his friend talk more soberly: the life of virtue is not concerned with such things as these. The fine passage which follows can scarcely be altogether ironical. "Riches and glory, and all pleasures of the body, all these are stripped off and left below, and the man ascends, like Hercules, who rose a god from the pile which consumed him on Mount Œta: so did he throw off there all that was mortal, all that he inherited from his earthly mother, and bearing with him that which was divine, now purified by fire and cleansed from all dross, soared upwards to the gods. And so they who are purified by philosophy, as though by fire, from the love of all those things which men in their ignorance hold in admiration, attain the summit and there enjoy all happiness, remembering no more either riches, or glory, or pleasure, and smiling at those who still believe in their existence."

Lycinus meets him with the weapon which is always at hand—which the weakness of human nature furnishes us with as an answer to all high aspirations. Men's lives are not found to be in accordance with the principles they profess. The actual Stoics whom he sees and knows do not display this insensibility to riches and pleasures which the theoretical Stoic proclaims. He has seen Hermotimus's own master, the great Stoic himself, dragging off a pupil before the magistrates for not paying his fees. The dialogue which follows is amusing.

Hermotimus. Ah! that fellow was a rascal, and very ungrateful in the matter of payment. My master never treated other people so (and there were many he had lent money to)—because, you see, they paid him the interest punctually.

Lycinus. But even suppose they never paid, my good fellow, what difference could it make to a man like him,—purified by philosophy, and not caring for what he had left behind—on Mount Œta, you know?

Herm. You don't suppose it was on his own account he troubled himself about it? He has a young family, and he would not like to see them come to want.

Lyc. But then, my good Hermotimus, he ought to bring them up in virtuous habits too—to be happy like him, and care nothing for money.

Herm. I really have no time now, Lycinus, to discuss such questions with you: I'm in a great hurry to get to his lecture, and am afraid of being too late.

Lycinus begs him to set his mind at rest on that point; to-day, he can assure him, will be a holiday so far as lectures are concerned. He has just seen a notice to that effect, in large letters, posted on the professor's door. He happens to know that the excellent man is keeping his bed, and has given strict orders not to be disturbed; having, in fact, been at a late supper-party the night before, where he had eaten and drunk rather more than was good for him. He had been engaged there, too, in a warm dispute with a Peri patetic, which had helped to disturb his digestion. The scholar is naturally anxious to know whether his master got the better of his opponent. "Yes," says his informant; "the Peripatetic being rather obstinate and argumentative, not willing to be convinced and troublesome to refute, your excellent master, having a cup in his hand such as would have rejoiced the heart of old Nestor,* broke his head with it—they were sitting close together—and so silenced him at once." "An excellent plan, too," says the scholar; "there's no other way of dealing with men who won't be convinced." And Lycinus gravely assures him that he quite concurs in the opinion. "It is extremely wrong and foolish," he admits, "to provoke a philosopher—especially when he happens to have a heavy goblet in his hand."

He proposes, however, that as Hermotimus cannot go to his master's lecture to-day, he should turn lecturer himself for once, so far at least as to give his old friend some account of his experience as a student of philosophy. Only one thing he would be glad to

* "Scarce might another raise it from the board
When full; but aged Nestor raised with ease."
—Iliad, xi. 635 (Lord Derby).

know before they begin—will he permit his present ignorant pupil to ask questions, or even contradict him, if he sees occasion? Hermotimus says it is not usually allowed by the teacher, but in the present case he shall not object.*

The portion of this dialogue which follows is a clever imitation of the Socratic mode of argument by asking continuous questions, and forcing answers from an opponent which have the result of reducing his statement to an absurdity. Lycinus shows himself an adept in this kind of fence. Though too long for extract here, it is doing scanty justice to the author to condense it; yet the spirit of it may perhaps be fairly given.

Is there one only path to philosophy—that of the Stoics—or, as Lycinus has heard, many, and under various names? Many, undoubtedly, is the answer. —And do all teach the same or different? Totally different.—Then, probably, only one can be right? Certainly.—And how came Hermotimus (being at the first outset an ignoramus, of course, like others, and not the wise or half-wise man he is now)—how came he to know which to choose out of all these different schools? how distinguish the true from the false? Well—he saw the greater numbers go one way, and judged that must be the best.—And what majority had the Stoics over the Epicureans? and does he

* The disciples of Plato were apt to reply to those disputants who were so unreasonable as to ask for proof of any assertion—"He said it himself"—the "*ipse dixit*" which has passed into a modern phrase.

really think that in such a matter it is safe to go by a mere majority of voices? But it was not only that; he heard everybody say the Stoics were the wisest—that your true Stoic is the only complete man—king, and cobbler all in one.—Did the Stoics say this of themselves? (because you can hardly trust a man's own account of himself;) or did other people say it of them? Other people, also, certainly—many of them.—Surely not the philosophers of rival sects? they would not say so? No.—It was people who were not philosophers at all, then? the vulgar and illiterate, in fact? and could a man of sense like Hermotimus really go by what *they* said on such a question? Nay, but he had acted on his own judgment as well: he had observed the Stoics to be always grave and well-behaved, and respectably dressed; not effeminate like some, or rough like others. Then, says Lycinus, it comes to this, —you judge wisdom by dress, and looks, and gait: which makes it hard for the blind man, does it not? how is *he* to know which to follow? Hermotimus does not consider himself bound to make provision for the blind: that is an extreme case. Well, suppose we leave the blind to shift without philosophy, says Lycinus—though they seem to want it as much as anybody, poor fellows, to help them to bear their infirmity—still, even those who can see, how can they look inside a man and know what he really is? because you chose these men as guides, I suppose, for their insides, not their outsides? The student feels that he is no match for his opponent, and wants to close the discussion. "Nothing that I say satisfies you," he sulkily exclaims. "Nay," says the other, "you don't *try* to satisfy me. You want to go and leave me here in the slough of my ignorance: you are afraid lest I should become as good a philosopher as yourself. You won't teach me. So now you must listen to me—only don't laugh at my awkward way of putting things." The passage which follows is too fine to mutilate.

Lycinus. I picture virtue to myself in this way,—as it were a city whose inhabitants are perfectly happy (as your teacher would surely tell us if he could come down from thence), perfectly wise and brave and just and temperate, little less than gods. And in that city you would see none of those deeds which are common here among us—men robbing and committing violence, and overreaching each other: but they live together as fellow-citizens in peace and harmony. And no wonder; for all those things which in other states cause strife and contention, and for the sake of which men plot against each other, are put far away from them: for they regard neither gold, nor sensual pleasure, nor glory, not holding such things necessary to their polity. Thus they lead a calm and entirely happy life, under good laws and with equal rights, liberty, and all other blessings.

Hermotimus. Well, then, Lycinus, is it not good for all men to wish to be citizens of such a city, and neither to regard the toil of the road, nor the long time spent in the pilgrimage, so only they may reach it, and be enrolled on its records and share its privileges?

Lyc. Ay, verily it is, Hermotimus. That would of all things be best worth striving for, even if we had to give up all besides. Nor, though this present land in which we live should seek to hold us back, ought we to regard it; nor, though children or parents, if we have them, should seek with tears to detain us here, ought we to be moved by them, but rather, if we may, urge them to follow us on the same path, and if they cannot or will not, then shake ourselves free from them, and make straight for that blessed city—casting off our very garment, if they cling to that to retain us,—eager only to get there: for there is no fear, believe me, that even the naked should be denied admittance if they reach the gate. There was an old man, I remember, once on a time, who discoursed to me of how matters went in that city, and exhorted me to follow him thither: he would lead the way, he said, and when I came, would enrol me in his own tribe, and let me share his privileges, and so I should live happy there with them all. But I, in my youthful folly (I was scarce fifteen), would not listen to him, or I might now be in the suburbs of that city, or even at its gates.* Many things he told me of it, as I seem to remember, and among them this,—that all there were strangers and immigrants, and that many

* We shall never know Lucian's full meaning here. Is this but another version of "The Dream," and does he imply that he had failed to carry out the nobler ideal of his choice, and had sunk into the mere hired pleader? Or had he some higher "dream" still in his youth, whose invitation he was conscious of having disobeyed?

barbarians and slaves, nay, and deformed persons, and dwarfs, and beggars, were enrolled among its citizens, and in short, that any might win the freedom of that city who would. For that the law there was that a man should be ranked not by his dress, or his station, or his beauty, nor yet by his birth and noble ancestry: of such matters they took no account. But it sufficed, in order to become a citizen, that a man should have sense, and a love of the right, and diligence, and energy, and should not faint or be discouraged under the many difficulties he met with on the road: so that he who displayed these qualities, and made good his way thither, was at once admitted as a citizen with equal rights, be he who he might: and such terms as higher or lower, noble or plebeian, bond or free, were never so much as named in that community.

Herm. You see then, Lycinus, it is no vain or weak aspiration of mine, to become a denizen myself of such a noble and blessed republic.

Lyc. Nay, I also, my friend, have the same longing as yourself, and there is no blessing I would more devoutly pray for. If only that city were near, and manifest to all men's eyes, be sure that I had long ere this become a citizen of it. But since, as you say (both you and Hesiod), it lies far off, we must needs inquire the way, and seek the best guide we can,—is it not so?

Herm. Else we shall hardly get there.

Lyc. Now, so far as promises and professions of knowing the road go, we have guides offering themselves in plenty: many there are, who stand ready, who tell us they are actually natives of the place. But it would seem there is not one road thither, but many, and all in different directions—one east, one west, one north, another south; some lead through pleasant meadows and shady groves, with no obstacles or unpleasantness; others over rough and stony ground, through much heat and thirst and toil; yet all are said to lead to that one and the same city, though their lines lie so far apart.

There are guides, too, each recommending their own path as the only true one; which of all such are we to follow? There is Plato's road, and Epicurus's road, and the road taken by the Stoics; who is to say which is right? The guides themselves know no road but their own: and though each may declare that they have seen *a* city at the end of it, who knows whether they mean the *same* city, after all? The only safe guide would be the man who had tried every path,—who had studied profoundly all the theories of Pythagoras, Plato, Epicurus, Chrysippus, Aristotle, and the rest, and chosen that which, from his own knowledge and experience, he found to be the best and safest. And what lifetime would suffice for this? "Twenty years," says his friend to Hermotimus, "you have already been studying under the Stoics, you told us; and some twenty more you thought you required to perfect yourself in their philosophy. And how many would you give to Plato? and how many to Aristotle? and how long do you expect to live?"

Poor Hermotimus is no match for his Socratic cross

examiner. He declares, with great truth and honesty, that his clever friend has succeeded, like many clever disputants, in making him, at all events, very uncomfortable, and that he heartily wishes he had never met him that morning in his quiet meditations. "You always were overbearing in argument, Lycinus; I don't know what harm Philosophy ever did you, that you hate her so, and make such a joke of us philosophers." "My dear Hermotimus," calmly replies his friend, "you and your master, being philosophers, ought to know more about Truth than I do: I only know this much,—she is not always pleasant to those who listen to her."

The Dialogue is extended to some length, but the neophyte Stoic fails to hold his ground. Lycinus argues that after all there comes no answer to that great question—'What is truth?' It may be, after all, that she is something different from anything yet discovered. All visions of her are but different guesses, and all the guesses may be wrong. And life is too short to waste in interminable speculations. "Words, words," are, in the opinion of Lycinus, the sum of the philosophy of the day, whereas life demands action. Hermotimus becomes convinced that he has hitherto been wasting his time; henceforth he will try to do his duty as a private citizen, and if he meets a professor of philosophy in the street, will "avoid him as he would a mad dog."

Lucian is best remembered as a satirist and a jester, but this Dialogue is enough to prove to us that he was something more. He jests continually at the falsehoods which were passed off as Truth, and at the doubtful shadows, of various shape and hue, which confident theorists insisted were her true and only embodiment. But if he could have been sure of her identity, there is no reason to think he would not have become her ready and willing worshipper.

THE NEW ICARUS.

Hopelessly puzzled by the contradictory theories of the philosophers, especially on cosmogony, the Cynic Menippus has taken a journey to the stars to see whether he may possibly learn the truth there; and in the Dialogue which bears the above title he gives an account of his aerial travels to a friend. He had made for himself a rather uneven pair of wings by cutting off one from an eagle and one from a vulture, and after some preliminary experiments in flying had succeeded in making good his first stage, to the Moon. The earth and its inhabitants looked wonderfully small from that height; indeed, except the Colossus of Rhodes and the watch-tower of Pharos, he could make out little or nothing; until Empedocles, whom he met there (looking as black as a cinder, as well he might, having so lately come out of the crater of Ætna), showed him that by using the eagle's wing only for a while he might also acquire the eagle's vision. Then he saw many things not clearly discernible to ordinary eyes, for his new sight penetrated even into the houses. He saw the Epicurean forswearing himself for a thousand drachmas, the Stoic quarrelling with his pupils about fees, and the Cynic in very bad company. For the rest, the world was going on much as he supposed; the Egyptians were busy cultivating their fields, the Phœnicians making their merchant voyages, the Spartans whipping their children, and the Athenians, as usual, in the law-courts.* "Such," says the traveller, "is the confused jumble of this world. It is as though one should hire a multitude of singers, or rather bands of singers, and then bid each performer choose his own tune, caring nothing for the harmony; each singing his loudest, and going on with his own song, and trying to drown his neighbour's voice—you may judge what music that would make. Even such, my friend, are the performers on earth, and such is the confused discord which makes up human life; they not only sound different notes, but move in inharmonious time and figure, with no common idea or purpose; until the choir-master drives them all from the stage, and says he has no more need of them." He wondered, too, and could not forbear smiling, at the quarrels which arise between men about their little strips of territory, when to his eyes, as he looked down, "all Greece was but four fingers' breadth." It reminded him of "a swarm of ants running round and round and in and out of their city,—one turning over a bit of dung, another seizing a bean-shell, or half a

* A reminiscence of Aristophanes, who is never weary of satirising the passion of his fellow-citizens for law. In his "Clouds" (l. 280), where Strepsiades is shown Athens on the map, he exclaims—

"Athens! go to! I see no law-courts sitting."

grain of wheat, and running away with it. Probably among them too, conformably to the requirements of ant-life, they have their architects, and their popular leaders, and public officers, and musicians, and philosophers." [If his friend disapproves of the comparison, he bids him remember the old Thessalian fable of the Myrmidons.]

He was just taking flight again, he says, when the Moon—in a soft and pleasant female voice—begged him to carry something for her up to Jupiter. "'By all means,' said I, 'if it's not very heavy.' 'Only a message,' said she—'just a small petition to him. I'm quite out of patience, Menippus, at being talked about in such a shameful way by those philosophers, who seem to have nothing else to do but speculate about me —what I am, and how big I am, and why I am sometimes halved and sometimes round. Some of them say I'm inhabited, and others, that I hang over the sea like a looking-glass; in short, any fancy that comes into their heads, they apply to me. And, as if that were not enough, they say my very light is not my own, but as it were of a bastard sort, borrowed from the sun; trying to make mischief between me and him—my own brother—on purpose to set us at variance; as if it was not enough for them to say what they have about him, —that he is a stone, and nothing but a mass of fire. How many stories *I* could tell of *them*, and their goings-on o' nights, for all the grave faces and severe looks they wear by day! I see it all, though I hold my tongue—it seems to me scarcely decent to bring all their proceedings to light. So, when I see any of them misbehaving, I just wrap myself in a cloud, not to expose them. Yet they do nothing but discuss me in their talk, and insult me in every way. So that I swear I have often had thoughts of going away altogether as far as possible, to escape their troublesome tongues. Be sure you tell Jupiter this, and say besides, that I can't possibly stay where I am, unless he crushes those physical science men, gags the Dialecticians, pulls down the Porch, burns the Academy, and puts a stop to those Peripatetics: so that I may have a little peace, instead of being measured and examined by them every day.' 'It shall be done,' said I, and so took my leave."

So he went on, and reached the abode of Jupiter, where he hoped at first to get in without notice, being almost half an eagle—that bird being under Jupiter's protection; but, remembering that, after all, he was also half a vulture, he thought it best to knock at the door, which was opened by Mercury.* Jupiter complimented him highly upon his courage in making the journey, though the other gods were rather alarmed, thinking it a bad precedent for mortals. The monarch of Olympus asked him a good many questions as to the goings-on below, about which he appeared somewhat curious;—"What the price of wheat was now? What sort of a winter they had last year?" Especially he was anxious to know what mortals really thought about him. Menippus was very diplomatic in his answers. "'What can they

* Lucian evidently has in mind Trygæus's reception by Mercury, in the "Peace" of Aristophanes, i. 180, &c.

think, your majesty,' said I, 'but what they are in duty bound to think,—that you are the sovereign of the gods.' 'Nonsense,' replied his majesty; 'I know very well how fond they are all of something new. There was a time when I was thought good enough to give them oracles, and heal their diseases, —when Dodona and Pisa were in all their glory, and looked up to by everybody, and so full of sacrifices that I could hardly see for the smoke. But ever since Apollo set up his oracle at Delphi, and Æsculapius his surgery at Pergamus, and Bendis has had her worship in Thrace, and Anubis in Egypt, and Diana at Ephesus, they all run there to hold their festivals and offer their hecatombs, and look upon me as old-fashioned and decrepit, and think it quite enough to sacrifice to me once in six years at Olympia.'" They had a good deal more chat together, says Menippus, after which Jupiter took him to see the place where the prayers came up—through holes with covers to them. Their purport was various and contradictory: one sailor praying for a north wind, another for a south; the farmer for rain, and the fuller for sunshine. Jupiter only let the reasonable prayers come through the hole, and blew the foolish ones back again; but was sadly puzzled by the contradictory petitions,—especially when both petitioners promised him a hecatomb. This business over, they went to supper; and Menippus was highly delighted with Apollo's performance on the harp, with Silenus's dancing, and with the recitation of some of Hesiod's and Pindar's poetry by the

Muses. A general council of the gods was afterwards called, in which Jupiter announced his intention of making very short work with the philosophers of whom the Moon had complained. Then Menippus was dismissed, under the charge of Mercury, who had orders, however, to take off his wings, that he might not come that way again; and he is now hurrying, he tells his friend, with some malicious enjoyment, to warn the gentlemen of the Schools of what they may very soon expect from Jupiter.

CHAPTER V.

SATIRES ON SOCIETY:

THE PARASITE—UPON HIRED COMPANIONS.

It needs but a slight acquaintance with Greek and Roman literature, and with social life at Athens in its later days, and at Rome in the times of the emperors, to know that the men of rank and wealth filled their tables not only with their private friends, but also with guests who stood lower in the social scale, and were invited because they contributed in some way either to the amusement of the company or to the glorification of the host. A rich man, if he had any pretence to a good position in society, kept almost open house: and there was a class of men who, by means of sponging and toadying, and all those kindred arts which are practised, only under somewhat finer disguises, in modern society, contrived seldom either to go without a dinner or to dine at home. This disreputable fraternity of diners-out—"Parasites," as the Greek term was—supplied an inexhaustible subject for the satirist and the play-writer, as has been already noticed in these volumes, in examining the comedies of Plautus and Terence. Lucian has not omitted to handle, in his own style, a character so well known, and which presented such fair game to the writer who set himself to hunt down the follies of the times. Yet the little dialogue called "THE PARASITE," in which he introduces one of these mendicants of society arguing stoutly in defence of his vocation, is one of the most good-humoured of all. Perhaps there was an amount of *bonhomie* about a man who could not afford to be disagreeable which disarmed the satirist, together with a serio-comic "poor-devil" misery inevitable to his position which excited pity as well as contempt. Few readers can lay down the "Phormio" of Terence without a kindly feeling towards its unabashed and ingenious hero.

Simo, the Parasite of Lucian's Dialogue, makes open profession of his vocation, like Phormio. The friend with whom the conversation is carried on, knowing that Simo's private means are small, is curious to know by what trade or employment he gains his living, since he cannot make out that he follows any. Simo assures him that there is a school of art in which he is a perfect master, and which never allows him to be in want. It is the art of Parasitism. And he proceeds to prove, by an argument in the catechetical style of Socrates and Plato, that it is an art of the highest and most perfect kind. It falls quite within the definition of art as given by the philosophers—"a system of approved rules co-operating to a certain end, useful to society." As to the usefulness of the end, nothing is so useful—nay, so absolutely needful—as eating and drinking. It is not a gift of nature, but acquired, therefore an art, if the schoolmen be right in their technical distinctions. It is also most practical, which is the essence of a perfect art: other arts may exist in their possessor *in posse*, yet be seldom or never in operation; whereas this must be always at work—for when the parasite ceases to get his dinners, there is an end, not only of the art, but of the artificer. It excels all other arts also in this,—that whereas most arts require toil and discipline, and even threats and stripes, in order to be learnt thoroughly—which things are manifestly contrary to our nature—this art can be studied pleasantly and cheerfully without any of these disagreeable accompaniments. "Who ever yet returned in tears from a feast, as many scholars do from their masters? Who that is going to a good dinner ever looks pale and melancholy, as those do who frequent the Schools?" Other arts we pay to learn, this we are paid for learning; others require a master, this may be learnt without. Other systems seem vague; all give different definitions of wisdom and happiness—and that which is so indefinite can have no real existence at all; whereas the end and object of Parasitism is distinct and obvious. And in this alone of all systems the practice of the school agrees with its professions. And whereas no parasite was ever known to desert his art and turn philosopher, many philosophers have turned parasites, and do so to this day. Euripides became the dependant of Archelaus of Macedon; and even Plato was content to sit at the table of the tyrant Dionysius. If the testimony of the wise men of old is to be taken in evidence of the value and antiquity of the art, look only at Homer, a witness whom, the speaker hopes, every one will admit. He makes some of his greatest heroes parasites—old Nestor, always a guest at the table of the King of Men, and Patroclus, who was nothing more or less than the parasite of Achilles, and whom it took the combined power of two mortal warriors and a god to kill,* whereas Paris alone proved a match for his master Achilles, as Achilles had for Hector. Listen, he says, to the poet's own words touching this great school of the table :—

> " Find me a joy to human heart more dear
> Than is a people's gladness, when good cheer
> Reigns, and all listening pause in deep delight,
> When in mid feast the bard his song doth rear,
> What time the board with all good things is dight."

And, as if this were not praise enough, he adds again—

> " Methinks that nothing can more lovely be ! " †

By such ingenious arguments, not at all an unfair burlesque upon the style of Plato and Aristotle, Simo succeeds in convincing his friend of the superiority in every way of the art which he himself follows with so much success. His listener determines to come to him for instruction, and hopes, as he is his first pupil, that he will teach him gratis.

But besides this lower class of parasites, who sought

* Euphorbus, Hector, and Apollo. See Iliad, xvi.
† Odyss., ix. 5, &c.

a precarious dinner from day to day by making themselves agreeable or useful to their entertainers, the great men of the day were in the habit of receiving at their tables as daily guests, or even of entertaining altogether as members of their household,—often in the really or professed capacity of tutors to their sons,—guests of a different stamp. The man of wealth and position hardly thought his establishment complete, unless it comprised some of the representatives of literature and science—a philosopher or two, a poet, a rhetorician, or a historian. There was not necessarily anything degrading in the arrangement to the recipient of such hospitality. He might consider himself as the rightful successor of the bard of olden times, whose divine song was more than payment for his place at the feast, and to whom, by prerogative of genius, the highest seat at the king's board, and the best portion from the king's table, was by all willingly accorded. On such terms we may suppose that Plato, in spite of Simo's sarcasm, lived at the court of Dionysius; and with a scarcely less independent feeling, Horace would tell us that he accepted the gracious welcome of Mæcenas. But guests of the calibre of Plato and Horace were few; and men who had neither the munificence of Dionysius nor the taste of Mæcenas yet wanted to have the Muses represented at their banquets. If one was not a philosopher or a poet or play-writer one's self, at least it was well, since such things were the fashion, to be in the fashion so far as to have them in the house. If it was as troublesome for the rich man to do his own thinking for himself as the oriental would consider it to do his own dancing, it was desirable to have it done for him. A swarm of small sciolists, and worse than mediocre poets, and *littérateurs* of all varieties, rose to meet the demand, and sought places at great men's tables. Conscious that their services were scarcely worth the wages, they learnt to be not too fastidious as to the circumstances under which they were paid: while the patron, feeling that after all he had not got the genuine article, was not always careful to make the payment in the most gracious manner.

With this in his mind, Lucian writes his bitter essay "UPON HIRED COMPANIONS," cast in the form of a letter to a friend who is supposed to be under some temptation to adopt that line of life. He draws a vivid picture of the humiliations and indignities to which the Greek scholar is likely to be subjected who enters the family of a wealthy nobleman at Rome, in the capacity either of tutor to his children or humble literary companion to the master himself. They are curiously similar in character to those which, if we trust our own satirists, existed in English society a century ago. First, there is the difficulty of securing a proper introduction to the patron. The candidate must be early at the great man's door, and wait his leisure, and fee the porter well; must dress more expensively than his purse can well afford, to make a good figure in his eyes; must dance attendance at his levee perhaps for days, and at last, when he suddenly condescends to notice and address his humble servant, nervousness and embarrassment will so overcome the unfortunate man, that he makes an absolute fool of himself in the interview which he has so anxiously desired, and leaves an impression of nothing but awkwardness and ignorance.

But, pursues the letter-writer, supposing that your introduction is successful: supposing that the great man's friends do not set him against you, that the lady of the house does not take a violent dislike to you, that the steward and the housekeeper are graciously pleased to approve of you on the whole,—still, what an ordeal you have to go through at your very first dinner!

"My lord's gentleman, a suave personage, brings you the invitation. You must win his goodwill, to begin with: so, not to seem wanting in good manners, you slip five drachmæ into his hand, at the least. He affects to refuse it. 'From you, sir? Oh dear, no! on no account—I couldn't think of it.' But he is persuaded at last, and smiles with his white teeth as he takes his leave. Well, you put on your best suit, and get yourself up as correctly as you can, and reach the door—very much afraid of arriving before the other guests, which is as awkward as coming last is rude. So you take careful pains to hit the happy medium, are graciously received, and are placed within a few seats of the host,—just below two or three old friends of the house. You stare at everything as if you had been introduced all at once into the palace of Jupiter, and watch every detail anxiously—all is so new and strange; while the whole family have their eyes on you, and are watching what you will do next.

Indeed the great man has even given orders to some of the attendants to take notice whether you seem to admire his wife and children sufficiently. Even the servants of the other guests who are present notice your evident embarrassment, and laugh at your ignorance of the ways of society, guessing that you have never been to a regular dinner-party before, and that even the napkin laid for you is something quite new to you. No wonder that you are actually in a cold sweat from embarrassment, and neither venture to ask for drink when you want it, for fear they should think you a hard drinker, or know which to take first and which last of the various dishes which are arranged before you evidently in some kind of recognised sequence and order. So that you are obliged furtively to watch and imitate what your next neighbour does, and so make yourself acquainted with the ceremonial of dinner."

"Such," says the letter-writer, after a little more description of the same kind,—"such is your first dinner in a great man's house: I had rather, for my part, have an onion and some salt, and be allowed to eat it when and how I please." Then come the delicate arrangements about salary. When one reads Lucian's description of this, it is almost difficult to believe that he had not before him one of those modern advertisements for a governess, who is expected to possess all the virtues and all the accomplishments, and to whom "a very small salary is offered, as she will be treated as one of the family." "We are quite plain people here, as you see," says the pompous Roman to the new tutor; "but you will consider yourself quite at home with us, I hope. I know you are a sensible man: I know you have that happy disposition which is its own best reward, and quite understand that you do not enter my house from any mercenary motives, but for other reasons,—because you know the regard I have for you, and the good position it will give you in the eyes of the world. Still, some definite sum should be fixed, perhaps. I leave it to you to name your own terms; remembering, of course, that you will have a good many presents made you in the course of the year: but you scholars, as becomes your profession, are above mere money considerations, I know." At last it is agreed to leave the amount of the tutor's salary to a friend of the family; and the referee, a mere creature and toady himself, after reminding the poor scholar of his extreme good fortune in having made "such a valuable connection," names a sum which is quite ridiculously inadequate.

This is not the worst. The unhappy dependant will soon find his treatment in the house very different from his first introduction. "You must not expect to have the same fare as strangers and others have: that would be considered insufferable presumption. The dish placed before you will not be the same as the others. Their fowl will be plump and well fed: yours will be half a skinny chicken, or a dry tough pigeon; a direct slight and insult. Nay, often, if the bill of fare is scanty, and an additional guest comes in, the servant will actually take the dish from before you and give it to him; whispering familiarly in your ear

—'you're one of the family, you know.'* While they are drinking good old wine, you will be expected to swallow some muddy vapid stuff: and you will do well to drink it out of gold or silver goblets, that it may not be plain to all, from the colour of the liquor, how little respect is paid to you in the household. Even of this poor stuff you will not be allowed your fill; for often, when you call for it, the servant will pretend not to hear."

He warns him, also, that in such a household the preceptor or the poet will be held of less account than the flutist, or the dancing-master, or the Egyptian boy who can sing love-songs. And after all, do what he will, he will hardly please. If he preserves a grave and dignified behaviour, he will be called churlish and morose; if he tries to be gay, and puts on a smiling face, the company will only stare and laugh at him.

If the town life of the unfortunate dependant is full of such mortifications, matters do not mend much when he accompanies his patron into the country. "Amongst other things, if it rains ever so hard, you must come last (that is your recognised place), and wait for a conveyance; and, if there is no room, be

* Lucian is not very original here. He had probably read the fifth Satire of Juvenal, where, among other indignities offered to the poor dependant, even the bread set before him is of very inferior quality—

> "Black mouldy fragments wh'ch defy the saw,
> The mere despair of every aching jaw,
> While manchets of the finest flour are set
> Before your lord."—Gifford.

crammed into the litter with the cook and my lady's woman, with scarce straw enough to keep you warm." And the writer goes on to relate a veritable anecdote, told him, as he declares, by a Stoic philosopher who had been so unfortunate as thus to hire himself out into the service of a rich Roman lady. The story reads almost like a bit out of Swift. Travelling one day into the country in the suite of his patroness, he found a seat allotted him next a perfumed and smooth-shaven gentleman who held an equivocal position in the lady's household, and whose bearing might answer to that of the French dancing-master of modern satirists; not a very suitable companion for the grave philosopher, who rather prided himself on a venerable beard and dignified deportment. Just as they were starting, the lady, with tears in her eyes, appealed to his known kindness of heart to do her a personal favour. Even a philosopher could not refuse a request couched in such terms. "Will you then so far oblige me," said she, "as just to take my dear little dog Myrrhina with you in the carriage, and nurse her carefully? She is not at all well, poor dear—in fact, very near her accouchement; and those abominable careless servants of mine will give themselves no trouble about me,—much less about her." So, during the whole journey, there was the little beast peeping out of the grave philosopher's cloak, yelping at intervals, and now and then licking his face, and making herself disagreeable in divers ways; giving occasion to his companion to remark, with a mincing wit, that he had become a *Cynic* philosoper instead of a Stoic for the present." * Those who liked to make a good story complete declared afterwards to the present narrator that the philosopher, before they reached their journey's end, found himself nurse to a litter of puppies as well as to their interesting mother.

Scarcely less distasteful is the duty which belongs to the literary companion of listening to his patron's compositions, if he is a dabbler, as so many are, in poetry, or history, or the drama, since one must not only listen but loudly applaud his wretched attempts as an author. Or, where the companion is expected himself to give readings of his own to amuse the leisure of his patron, the mortification may be even greater—especially if, as in the case just mentioned, the patron be of the softer sex. "It will often happen that while the philosopher is reading, the maid will bring in a billet from a lover. Straightway the lecture upon wisdom and chastity is brought to a stand-still, until the lady has read and answered the missive, after which they return to it with all convenient speed." †

* It is hardly necessary to repeat that the term "Cynic" is derived from the Greek for "dog."

† Some readers will remember the anecdote told of Dr ——, one of Queen Anne's chaplains. His duty was to read the Church prayers in the anteroom, while the queen was at her toilet within. Occasionally the door was shut, "while her majesty was shifting herself," during which interval the doctor left off, and resumed when the door was reopened. The other chaplains had not been so fastidious ; and the doctor was asked by one of her majesty's women, why he did not go straight on with his reading : upon which he replied that he "would never whistle the Word of God through a key-hole."

The writer entreats his friend to have too much self-respect to adopt a line of life so utterly distasteful to any man of independent spirit. "Is there no pulse still growing," he asks indignantly,—"no wholesome herbs on which a man may sustain life, no streams of pure water left, that you should be driven to this direst strait for existence?" If a man will deliberately choose such a life, he bids him not rail at his fate hereafter, as many do, but remember those words of Plato,—"Heaven is blameless—the fault lies in our own choice."

It must be borne in mind that we here are reading satire, and not social history, and that it would be unfair to judge of the common position of literary men in the houses of the great from this highly coloured sketch of Lucian's. No doubt there were still to be found hosts like Mæcenas wherever there were companions like Horace. Few readers can have followed these extracts from Lucian's description of the literary dependant of his own day, without having forcibly recalled to them Macaulay's well-known picture of the domestic chaplain of the days of the Stuarts. There is abundant material for that brilliant caricature to be found, of course, in the satirists and the comedy-writers of those times,—the Lucians of the day; and they no doubt could have pointed to the original of every feature in their portraits. It does not follow that such portraits are to be taken as fair representatives of a class. But we must remember that the lively author we have now before us did not profess to be writing history; and it is well not to forget in reading the English historian's pages that we are following Oldham and Swift.

THE MARVEL-MONGERS.

We have seen the bitter and unsparing ridicule which, not without a purpose, Lucian brings to bear against the fables which passed under the name of religion in his day. But, if he laughed at Greek mythology, he hated the strange and outlandish superstitions which he saw creeping in at Athens and at Rome. He threw something of his own feeling into the remonstrance of the "old families" of Olympus, when they saw dog-headed monsters like Anubis, and apes and bulls from Memphis, introduced into the sacred circle. We have no need to depend upon satirists like Horace, or Juvenal, or Lucian—we need only go to the pages of the historian Tacitus—to learn how the superstitions of Egypt and Asia were gaining favour with the aristocracy of Rome. "Never," says Wieland, "was the propensity to supernatural prodigies and the eagerness to credit them more vehement than in this very enlightened age. The priestcraft of Upper Egypt, the different branches of magic, divination, and oracles of all kinds, the so-called occult sciences, which associated mankind with a fabulous world of spirits, and pretended to give them the control over the powers of nature, were almost universally respected. Persons of all ranks and descriptions—great lords and ladies, statesmen, scholars, the recognised and paid professors of the Pythagorean, the Platonic, the Stoic, and even the Aristotelian school, thought on these topics exactly as did the simplest of the people. . . . Men believed everything—and nothing."

It is in derision of this passion for the marvellous that Lucian composed this Dialogue between two friends, Tychiades and Philocles, of whom the former may be taken to represent the author himself. Tychiades wants to know why so many people prefer lies to truth? Well, replies his friend, in some cases men are almost obliged to tell lies for the sake of their own interest; and in war, lies to deceive an enemy are allowable. But some people, rejoins the other, seem to take a pleasure in lying for its own sake; and this is what puzzles him. Herodotus and Homer, so far as he can make out, were notorious liars; and lied withal in such a charming way, that their lies, unlike most others, have had immense vitality.

Philocles thinks something may be said in their defence: they were obliged, in order to be popular, to consult the universal taste for the marvellous. Besides, if all the old Greek fables are to be set aside, what is to become of the unfortunate people who get their living by showing the antiquities and curiosities?

Be this as it may, Tychiades has been quite shocked and astonished at what he has heard at a party lately given by his friend Eucrates—a grey-headed philosopher, who at least ought to have known better. He was laid up with gout; and the lying absurdities which his friends and physicians were prescribing for him by way of remedies were atrocious. A weasel's tooth wrapped in a lion's skin—though the doctors gravely squabbled whether it should not rather be a deer-skin—did any one ever hear the like? And then the guests had all set to work to tell the most marvellous stories—stories which go a long way to show how little novelty there is in the inventions of superstition; of magic rings made out of gibbet-irons; of haunted houses in which ghosts appeared and showed the way to their unburied bones; of a statue which at night stepped down from its pedestal and walked about the house, and even took a bath—you might hear him splashing in the water; of a slave who, having stolen his master's goods, was every night flogged by an invisible hand—you could count the wheals upon his back in the morning; of a little bronze figure of Hippocrates, only two spans high (this is the doctor's story), who is also given to nocturnal perambulations, and, small as he is, makes a great clatter in the surgery, upsetting the pill-boxes and changing the places of the bottles, if he has not had proper honour paid to him in the way of sacrifice during the year; of a colossal figure terminating in a serpent—Eucrates has seen it himself—before whose feet the infernal regions opened. Eucrates' own wife, again, whom he had burnt and buried handsomely, with all her favourite dresses too, in order to make her as comfortable as possible in her new state of existence,* had appeared to him seven months afterwards—"while I was lying on my couch,

* Probably founded on the story of Melissa's complaint to her husband Periander, that she was cold in the Shades below, because her clothes had only been buried, and not burnt, with her.—Herodotus, v. 92.

just as I am now, and reading Plato on the immortality of the soul" — and frightened him terribly. She had missed an article of her wardrobe — one of a pair of golden slippers to which she was particularly attached, and there was no rest for her perturbed spirit without it. Happily the slipper was found next morning in the very place which the lady had indicated, behind a chest, and was duly burned; and both husband and household had peace afterwards.

Eucrates had another story to tell also, of something which had happened to himself—a story with which we are tolerably familiar in more than one modern form, but which it may be amusing to read here in an older version. The narrator had the good fortune, on a voyage up the Nile, to make the acquaintance of a certain Pancrates, one of the holy scribes of Memphis, who had learnt magic from the goddess Isis herself. They became so intimate that they agreed to continue their travels together, Pancrates assuring his friend that they should have no need of servants.

"When we got to an inn, this remarkable man would take the bar of the door, or a broom, or a pestle, put some clothes on it, mutter a charm over it, and make it walk, looking to every one else's eyes for all the world like a man: it would go and draw water, fetch provisions and set them out, and make an excellent servant and waiter in all respects. Then, when its office was done to our contentment, he would mutter a counter-charm, and make the broom become a broom again, and the pestle a pestle. Now this charm I never could get him to disclose to me, with all my entreaties; he was jealous on this one point, though in everything else he was most obliging. But one day, standing in a dark corner, I overheard the spell —it was but three syllables—without his knowing it. He went off to market after giving the pestle its orders. So next day, when he was gone out on business, I took the pestle, dressed it up, and bid it go and draw water. When it had filled the pitcher and brought it back, "Stop!" said I; "draw no more water; be a pestle again." But it paid no attention to me, but went on drawing water till the whole house was full. Not knowing what on earth to do (for Pancrates was sure to be in a terrible way when he came back, as indeed fell out), I laid hold on a hatchet, and split the pestle in two. At once both halves took up a pitcher apiece, and began drawing water. So instead of one water-carrier, I had two. In the middle of it all, in came Pancrates, and understanding how matters stood, changed them back into wood again as they were before. But he went off and left me without a word, and I never knew what became of him."

They afterwards went on to tell so many horrible stories, that Tychiades left them in disgust; and he declares to his friend that even now he has nothing but goblins and spectres before his eyes ever since, and would give something to forget the conversation.

A passage occurs in this Dialogue worthy of remark,

as containing, in the opinion of some, one of the few notices of Christianity which occur in contemporary heathen writers. One of the party at which the narrator was present speaks of having been an eyewitness of certain cures worked upon "demoniacs" by a person of whom he speaks as "that Syrian from Palestine, whom all men know." "He would stand over those possessed, and ask the spirits from whence they had entered into the body? and the sick man himself would be silent, but the devil would reply, either in Greek or some barbarous tongue of his own country, how and from whence he had entered into the man. Then the exorcist, using adjurations, and, if these had no effect, even threats, would expel the spirit."* It has been thought that here we have a record of healing wrought by some one of the successors of the Christian apostles. It must be observed, however, that the cure is here expressly said to have been performed "for a large fee," and that we have distinct mention in the Acts of the Apostles of professed exorcists who were not Christians.

The "SATURNALIA," and the piece called "NIGRINUS," may also be classed with the preceding. In the first, the author takes occasion of the well-known annual festival, kept in remembrance of the "good old times," at which so much general licence was allowed even to slaves, to deal some good-humoured blows at the follies of the day; and at the same time to introduce Saturn

* "The Marvel-Mongers" (Philopseudes), 16.

himself as a poor gouty decrepit old deity, quite out of date, and to remark upon Jupiter's unfilial conduct in turning him out of his kingdom. In the latter Dialogue, a Platonic philosopher named Nigrinus (whether a real or imaginary personage is not certainly known) contrasts the pomp and luxury of Roman city life with the simpler habits of the Athenians.

CHAPTER VI.

LUCIAN AS A ROMANCE-WRITER.

We can readily see, from the spirit and vivacity of Lucian's Dialogues, what an admirable novelist he would have been; especially if he had chosen the style which has of late become deservedly popular, where nice delineation of character, and conversation of that clever and yet apparently natural and easy kind in which "the art conceals the art," form the attraction to the reader, rather than exciting incidents or elaborate plot. But this kind of literature had yet to be born. Lucian has left us, however, two short romances, if they may be so called, which it would be hardly fair to compare with modern works of fiction, but which show that he possessed powers of imagination admitting of large and successful development if his own age had afforded scope and encouragement to literary efforts of that kind. It must be remembered that the modern novel, in all its various types, is the special product of modern society; the love-tales which so largely form its staple, and the nice distinctions of character on which so much of its interest depends, spring entirely out of the circumstances of modern civilisation, and could have no place in Greek or Roman life in the days of Lucian. Yet he may fairly claim to have furnished hints, at least, of which later workers in the same field have taken advantage.

One of these tales Lucian has entitled "The Veracious History." Even here he preserves his favourite character of satirist; for he glances slyly, both in the opening of his story and throughout it, at the stories told by the old poets and historians, which he would have us understand are often about as "veracious" as his own. His old quarrel with the pretenders to philosophy breaks out also from time to time in the same pages. He introduces his story (which is the account of an imaginary voyage made into certain undiscovered regions) by a kind of preface, of which the following is a portion.

"Ctesias, son of Ctesiochus, of Cnidus, has written an account of India, and of the things there which he never either saw himself or heard from any one else. So also Iambulus has told us a great many incredible stories about things in the great ocean, which everybody knew to be false, but which he has put together in a form by no means unentertaining.* So many others besides, with the same end in view, have related what purported to be their own travels and adventures, describing marvellously large beasts and savage men, and strange modes of life. But the ring-

* Ctesias's 'Indica,' of which Photius gives an abridgment, though to some extent fabulous, is not so contemptible as Lucian represents. Iambulus, whose account of India Diodorus Siculus adopts, seems to have indulged in pure fiction.

leader and first introducer of this extravagant style is that Ulysses of Homer's, telling his stories at the court of Alcinöus, about the imprisonment of the winds, and the one-eyed Cyclops, and the man-eaters, and suchlike savage tribes; and about creatures with many heads, and the transformation of his comrades by magic potions, and all the rest of it, with which he astonished the simple Phæacians. When I read all these, I do not blame the writers so much for their lies, because I find the custom common even with those who pretend to be philosophers. All I wonder at is, that they should ever have supposed that people would not find out that they were telling what was not true. Wherefore, being myself incited (by an absurd vanity, I admit) to leave some legacy to posterity, that I may not be the only man without my share in this open field of story-telling, and having nothing true to tell (for I never met with any very memorable adventures), I have turned my thoughts to lying; in much more excusable fashion, however, than the others. For I shall certainly speak the truth on one point,—when I tell you that I lie; and so it seems to me I ought to escape censure from the public, since I freely confess there is not a word of truth in my story. I am going to write, then, about things which I never saw, adventures I never went through, or heard from any one else; things, moreover, which never were, nor ever can be. So my readers must on no account believe them."

The adventures of the voyagers "from the Pillars of Hercules into the Western Ocean" are indeed of the most extravagant kind. They have all the wild impossibilities without much of the picturesqueness of an Eastern tale. A burlesque resemblance is kept up throughout to the kind of incident which, in the mouths of the old bards, had passed for history. We read how they came to a brass pillar with an almost illegible inscription, marking the limit of the travels of Hercules and Bacchus, and found near it on a rock the prints of two footsteps, one "measuring about an acre"—plainly that of Hercules; the smaller one, of course, belonged to Bacchus: how they found rivers of native wine,—a manifest confirmation of the visit of the latter god to those parts: and how a whirlwind carried them, ship and all, up into the moon, where they made acquaintance with Endymion, and saw the earth below looking like a moon to them, which shows that Lucian was not so far wrong in his astronomy. How their ship was swallowed by a sea-monster, and they lived inside him a year and eight months, carrying on a small war against a previous colony whom they found established there: and effected their escape at last by lighting an enormous fire, so that the monster died of internal inflammation. After this they made their way to that hitherto undiscovered country, the 'Island of the Blest,' when they were bound in fetters of roses, and led before Rhadamanthus, the king. We have a glowing description of the city, with its streets of gold and walls of emerald, temples of beryl and altars of amethyst; where there was no day or night, but a perpetual luminous twilight; where it was always spring, and none but the south wind blew; and where the vines ripened their fruit every month.* There they found most of the heroes of Grecian legend and of later history. Philosophers, too—genuine philosophers—were there in good number. And here the satirist quite gets the mastery over the story-teller. Plato was remarked as absent; he preferred living "in his own Republic, under his own laws," to any Elysium that could be offered him. The Stoics had not yet arrived, when these voyagers reached the island, though they were expected; Hesiod's 'Hill of Virtue,'† which they all had to climb, was such a very long one. Neither were the Sceptics of the Academy to be seen there; they were thinking of coming, but had "doubts" about it—doubts whether there were any such place at all; and perhaps, thinks Lucian, they were shy of encountering the judgment of Rhadamanthus, having a profound dislike to any decisive judgment upon any subject whatever.

The travellers would gladly have remained in the Happy Island altogether, but this was not allowed. They were promised, however, by Rhadamanthus, that if during their further voyage they complied with certain rules, which remind us of the old burlesque oath for-

* It has been thought that the writer must either have seen or heard of the description of the New Jerusalem in the Revelation. But figurative diction has always some features in common; and in this passage reminiscences of the Greek poets are very evident. The ingenuity of some commentators has discovered, not only here, but throughout this "Veracious History," an intentional travesty of Scripture. But such an idea is surely fanciful.

† See p. 121.

merly sworn by travellers at Highgate—such as "never to stir the fire with a sword, and never to kiss any woman above two-and-twenty" *—they should in good time find their way there again. Just as the writer is taking his leave, "Ulysses, unknown to Penelope, slipped into his hand a note to Calypso, directed to the island of Ogygia." The note, in the course of their subsequent wanderings, was duly delivered, and Calypso entertained the bearers very handsomely in her island; asking, not without tears, many questions about her old lover; and also—whether Penelope was really so very lovely and so virtuous? to which, very prudently, says Lucian, "we made such a reply as we thought would please her best."

They meet with some other adventures, tedious to our ears, sated as they are with fiction in all shapes, but probably not so to the hearers or readers to whom Lucian addressed them. But either he grew tired of story-telling, or the conclusion of this "Veracious History" has been lost; for it breaks off abruptly,

* This latter caution bears a curious similarity to one of the parting injunctions which Perceval (or Peredur), when setting out from home in quest of adventures, receives from his mother, and which appears with little variation in the Welsh, Breton, and Norman legends—to kiss every demoiselle he meets, without waiting for her permission; it is, she assures him, a point of chivalry. He carries out his instructions, according to one *raconteur*, by kissing the first lady he falls in with "vingt fois," in spite of her resistance, pleading his filial obligation :

> "Ma mère m'enseigna et dit
> Que les pucèles saluasse
> En quel lieu que je les trovasse."
>
> —Chrestien de Troyes.

leaving some promises made in the early portion unfulfilled.

De Bergerac, in his 'Voyage to the Moon' and 'History of the Empire of the Sun,' Swift, in his 'Gulliver's Travels.' Quevedo, in his 'Visions,' and Rabelais, in his 'History of Gargantua and Pantagruel,' are all said to have borrowed from this imaginary voyage of Lucian's. But they can have taken from him little more than crude hints, and Swift at least owes a much larger debt to De Bergerac than to Lucian.

Lucius, or The Ass, is another short essay in fiction, complete in itself, and approximating more closely to our modern idea of a story. It relates the transformation of the hero into an ass, through the accidental operation of the charm of a sorceress, and his restoration, after a variety of adventures in his quadruped form, into his own proper shape by feeding on some roses. It is not certain whether the story is original, or merely an abridgment in our author's own style from a tale by one Lucius of Patræ. The "Golden Ass" of Apuleius (written probably at about the same date) seems to be founded either on this piece of Lucian's or on the common original, but Apuleius extends the tale to greater length. The experiences of Lucius in the person of the ass, while retaining all his human faculties, are fairly amusing, but not tempting either for extract or abridgment. The piece is chiefly interesting as one of the few surviving specimens of an ancient novelette.

Shorter, but much more amusing, is the pleasant

little sketch, cast in Lucian's favourite form of a Dialogue—"THE COCK AND THE COBBLER."

The Cobbler is our old friend Micyllus, who is awakened one morning much earlier than he likes by the crowing of his cock, whom he declares he would kill if it were not too dark to catch him. The Cock remonstrates: he is only doing his duty; and if his master will not get up and make a shoe before breakfast, he is very likely to go without. Micyllus is very much startled at the prodigy of a cock's finding a human voice; upon which the bird remarks that if Achilles's horse Xanthus could make a long speech, and in verse too, and the half-roasted oxen in the Odyssey could low even on the spit—and there is Homer's excellent authority for both *—surely he may say a few words in humble prose. Besides, if his master wants to know, he has not always been a bird—he was a man, once upon a time: Micyllus has surely heard of the great philosopher Pythagoras, and his transformations? Yes, Micyllus has heard all about it—and a great impostor he was. "Pray, don't use violent language," replies the Cock; "I am Pythagoras—or rather, I was." He proceeds to explain how many and various transmigrations he has already gone through; he has been a king, a beggar,

* It will be observed that Lucian is continually jesting upon the marvels related by Homer, and affecting to be shocked at them as palpable lies. But his very familiarity with the poet is proof sufficient of his real appreciation of him. Like the old angler, he puts him on his hook, but still "handles him tenderly, as though he loved him."

a woman, a horse, and a jackdaw; and never more miserable than in the character of a king. Micyllus expresses great surprise at this statement: for his own part, riches are the one thing he has always longed for; and the reason for his having been so angry now at being awakened was that he was in the midst of a most charming and interesting dream—it was, that he had inherited all the great wealth of his rich neighbour Eucrates, and was giving a grand supper on the occasion. He had thought he should now be able to repay the insolence of his former acquaintance Simo, who from a cobbler like himself had become suddenly a rich man, and would no longer recognise his old associate. The Cock assures his master that in his present poor estate he is really happier than many of the wealthy and great; and he will give him proof positive of his assertion. One of the two long feathers in his (the cock's) tail—the right-hand one—has the miraculous power of opening locks, and even making a passage through walls: he bids Micyllus pull it out. The cobbler pulls out both, to make sure, at which the Cock is very angry, until assured by his master that with one feather he would have looked very lop-sided. Armed with this talisman (the same which Le Sage has borrowed for his 'Diable Boiteux'), the pair fly through the sleeping city from house to house. They visit amongst others Simo and Eucrates: they find the former hiding his money, unable to sleep, in an agony for fear of thieves; and the latter cheated and betrayed by his wife and his servants. And the cobbler goes back home a wiser and more contented man.

CHAPTER VII.

LUCIAN AND CHRISTIANITY.

THE notices of Christianity to be found in heathen authors who were either contemporary with its great Founder, or who wrote during the early ages of the Christian Church, are so few, that even the slightest has an interest beyond what would otherwise be its historical importance. The rarity of such notices, and their general brevity and indistinctness, is apt to surprise us, until we recollect that Christianity did not for some time make that impression upon the heathen world which from our own point of view we might naturally expect. The Christians were long regarded as merely a sect within a sect, and that an insignificant and despised one: even historians like Tacitus and Suetonius saw in the "Christus" whom they both mention little more than a ringleader of turbulent Jews. Superstitions of all kinds and from all quarters were crowding in, as we may see even from Lucian's own pages, upon the ground which the priesthood of pagan Rome were striving to hold by making the national religion so "catholic" as to include the gods of as many other creeds as they could. Men believed, as Wieland says, "everything, and nothing." A new god or a new superstition more or less made not much impression on the popular mind. The very feeling to which St Paul appeals at Athens, their readiness to adopt even an "unknown God," is evidence of a latitudinarianism in such matters which at once gave hope of toleration, and opened a dreary prospect of indifference. And indifference was, no doubt, the feeling with which the Christians were widely regarded, unless when by some misrepresentation of their doctrines they were denounced as plotters against the throne or the life of the reigning emperor, and the populace was hounded on against them, as in more modern times against the Jews, as atheists, sorcerers, and enemies of the state.

The attitude of Lucian towards Christianity has been the subject of more discussion than that of any other heathen writer. He has written an account of the self-immolation of one Peregrinus or Proteus, about whose character and antecedents the learned are not quite agreed. If Lucian's history of him is to be trusted, he was a Hellespontine Greek, who, after a youth of great profligacy, had, either from conviction or more probably for selfish ends, become a Christian, had held high office in the Church, and attained a position of great influence in the body, combining the pretensions of a Cynic philosopher with those of a Christian priest. He had even suffered for his professed faith, and been imprisoned by the governor of Syria. But this imprisonment Lucian thinks he purposely sought in order to obtain notoriety, which object the governor was aware of, and disappointed him by setting him free. He afterwards travelled, supported, according to apostolic precedent, by his fellow-believers; but being detected in some profanation (apparently) of the Eucharist,* he threw off his profession, and returned to his old profligate life. Expelled from Rome by the authorities for his scandalous conduct there, he endeavoured without success to excite the people of Elis to revolt against the Roman Government; and at length, finding his popularity and influence on the wane, sought to restore it by giving out publicly that he would burn himself solemnly at the forthcoming Olympic games. This intention, strange to say, he actually carried into execution; whether from an insane desire for posthumous notoriety, or whether, hoping to be rescued at the last moment by his friends, he had gone too far to recede, is not at all clear from any version of the story.

Lucian was an eyewitness of this very remarkable spectacle, of which he gives an account in the shape of a letter to a friend, prefacing it with a short biographical sketch, touched in very dark colours, of a man whom he considers to have been, both in his life and death, a consummate impostor. These are the passages in which he speaks of the Christians :—

"About this time, Peregrinus became a disciple of that extraordinary philosophy of the Christians, having met with some of their priests and scribes in Palestine. He soon convinced them that they were all mere chil-

* Lucian's words are, "I believe it was eating certain food forbidden among them." This may have reference to the "meats offered to idols :" or he may very probably here, as elsewhere, confound Christians with Jews.

dren to him, becoming their prophet and choir-leader and chief of their synagogue, and, in short, everything to them. Several of their sacred books he annotated and interpreted, and some he wrote himself. They held him almost as a god, and made him their lawgiver and president.* You know they still reverence that great man, Him that was crucified in Palestine for introducing these new doctrines into the world. On this account Proteus was apprehended and thrown into prison, which very thing brought him no small renown for the future, and the admiration and notoriety which he was so fond of. For, during the time that he was in prison, the Christians, looking upon it as a general misfortune, tried every means to get him released. Then, when this was found impossible, their attention to him in all other ways was zealous and unremitting. From early dawn you might see widows and orphans waiting at the prison-doors; and the men of rank among them even bribed the jailors to allow them to pass the night with him inside the walls. Then they brought in to him there sumptuous meals, and read their sacred books together; and this good Peregrinus (for he was then called so) was termed by them a second Socrates. There came certain Christians, too, from some of the cities in Asia, deputed by their community to bring him aid, and to counsel and encourage him. For they are wonderfully ready whenever their public interest is concerned—in short, they grudge nothing; and so much money came in to Peregrinus at that

* The Greek word here used (προστατης) possibly means bishop. St Cyril calls St Paul and St Peter by that name.

time, by reason of his imprisonment, that he made a considerable income by it. For these poor wretches persuade themselves that they shall be immortal, and live for everlasting; so that they despise death, and some of them offer themselves to it voluntarily. Again, their first lawgiver taught them that they were all brothers, when once they had committed themselves so far as to renounce the gods of the Greeks, and worship that crucified sophist, and live according to his laws. So they hold all things alike in contempt, and consider all property common, trusting each other in such matters without any valid security. If, therefore, any clever impostor came among them, who knew how to manage matters, he very soon made himself a rich man, by practising on the credulity of these simple people."

We have in this passage a not very unfair account of the discipline and practice of the early Christians, taking into consideration that it is given by a cynical observer, who saw in this new phase of religion only one superstition the more. There is an evident and not unnatural confusion here and there between Christians and Jews; and it is not clear whether the "first lawgiver" is a vague idea of Moses, or of St Paul, or of Christ himself. But in the "widows" we plainly see those deaconesses, or whatever we may term them, of whom Phœbe at Cenchrea was one; the "sumptuous meals" are almost certainly the "love-feasts" of the Church; while in the reading of the sacred books we have one of the most striking features of their public worship. In the account of the prison-life of

Peregrinus, impostor if he were, we seem to be reading but another version of that of St Paul—of the "prayer that was made of the Church" for him—of the good Philemon and Onesiphorus, who "ministered to him in his bonds," and those of "the chief of Asia who were his friends." The whole passage, brief as it is, bears token of having been penned by a writer who, if not acquainted with the tenets and practices of the Christians of those days from personal observation and experience, had at least gained his information from some fairly accurate source.

Such a passage was sure to exercise the criticism of Christian scholars, and very conflicting theories have been set up as to its interpretation, as bearing upon the author's own relations and feelings towards Christianity. Some over-ingenious speculators, reading it side by side with his bitter satire on the accepted theology of Paganism, have fancied that they saw in it evidence that Lucian himself was a Christian—in disguise. That after boldly and openly attacking Polytheism, and exhibiting it in the most grotesque caricature, he cautiously, as one treading on perilous ground, and still in a tone of half-banter, opens to his readers a half-view of the new philosophy whose ideal republic is a grander scheme than Plato's—the "simple people," the leading features of whose polity are "universal brotherhood" and "community of goods."

Such a view was tempting, no doubt, to a clever scholar, from the very paradox which it involved. But, except as a paradox, it is hard to conceive its having been propounded. It was much more natural to take, as many honest theologians did take and hotly maintain, quite the opposite view of Lucian's feelings towards the new religion. And these could certainly produce better evidence in support of their opinion. They traced in the sceptical tone of his writings the voice of an enemy to all forms of religion, true as well as false. They called him loudly "atheist" and "blasphemer." Some of them invented, and probably told until they believed it, a story of his having met his death by being torn in pieces by dogs—as such impiety well deserved. And one—Suidas—went so far as to express the charitable hope and belief that his punishment did not end there, but is still proceeding.* In the passage which has been here quoted, they saw a sneer at the holiest mysteries. Yet surely no such interpretation is self-evident to any candid reader. It is a cold, unimpassioned statement; half serious and half satiric, as is Lucian's wont; but neither prejudiced nor malicious. We have nothing here like the bitterness of Fronto or Celsus, or the stern anathema which Tacitus, ranking Christianity among other hated introductions from the East, hurls against it as an "execrable superstition." The tenets of this obscure sect did seem to Lucian—the man of the

* Suidas shall express himself in his own Latin, and if any English reader does not understand him, he will have no great loss: "Quare et rabiei istius pœnas sufficientes in præsenti vita dedit, et in futurum hæres æterni ignis una cum Satana erit."—Life of Lucian, prefixed to Zuinger's edit., 1602.

world—"extraordinary;" nothing more or less, whatever irony some may find in the word. Even the term "crucified sophist," however offensive to our ears, had nothing necessarily offensive as used by the writer. The clever Greek has no special sympathy with the "simple people" who were content with bad security for their money, and proved such an easy prey to any designing adventurer; but all his contempt and wrath is reserved for the impostor who cheated them. On him, and not on the Christians, he pours it out unsparingly. Here is his account of Peregrinus's last moments. The great games were over, but the crowd still lingered at Olympia to see the promised spectacle. It was deferred from night to night, but at last an hour was appointed. Attended by a troop of friends and admirers (a criminal going to execution, says the merciless narrator, has usually a long train), Peregrinus approached the pile, which had been prepared near the Hippodrome.

"Then the more foolish among the crowd shouted, 'Live, for the sake of the Greeks!' But the more hard-hearted cried, 'Fulfil your promise!' At this the old man was not a little put out, for he had expected that they would surely all lay hold on him, and not let him get into the fire, but force him to live against his will. But this exhortation to 'keep his promise' fell on him quite unexpectedly, and made him paler than ever, though his colour looked like death before. He trembled, and became silent. . . . When the moon rose (for she, too, must needs look upon this grand sight) he came forward, clad in his usual dress, and followed by his train of Cynics, and specially the notorious Theagenes of Patræ, well fitted to play second in such a performance. Peregrinus, too, carried a torch: and approaching the pile—a very large one, made up of pitch-pine and brushwood—they lighted it at either end. Then the hero (mark what I say) laid down his scrip and his cloak, and the Herculean club he used to carry, and stood in his under garment—and very dirty it was. He next asked for frankincense to cast on the fire; and when some one brought it, he threw it on, and turning his face towards the south (this turning towards the south is an important point in the performance) he exclaimed, 'Shades of my father and my mother, be propitious, and receive me!' When he had said this, he leaped into the burning pile and was seen no more, the flames rising high and enveloping him at once."

Lucian goes on to say, that when the followers of Peregrinus stood round weeping and lamenting, he could not resist some jokes at their expense, which very nearly cost him a beating. On his way home he met several persons who were too late for the sight; and when they begged him to give them an account of it, he added to the story a few touches of his own: how the earth shook, and how a vulture* was seen soaring out of the flames, and crying, "I have left earth, and mount to Olympus!" These

* The vulture among birds was the general scavenger, as the dog among beasts; and Lucian perhaps imagines the soul of he Cynic naturally taking that form.

little embellishments of the fact were, as he assures his friend, repeated afterwards as integral parts of the story. Some time afterwards he had met "a grey-haired old man, whose beard and venerable aspect might have seemed to bespeak a trustworthy witness," who solemnly declared that he had seen Proteus after his burning, "all in white, wearing a crown of olive;" nay, that he had not long ago left him "alive and cheerful, walking in the Hall of the Seven Echoes."

This portion of the narrative has also given rise to considerable discussion. Those who could see in Lucian nothing but a scoffer, asserted that the whole story was fictitious, and that his sole intention was to ridicule and caricature the deaths of Christian martyrs. They noted in this account of the last moments of Peregrinus many circumstances apparently borrowed from the deaths of the famous martyrs of the times. The previous attempts at rescue and the bribing of the jailors have their exact parallels in the case of Ignatius, and the Christians in their dreams saw him walking about in a glorified shape; the "olive-crown" might be an embodiment of that "crown of victory" of which he spoke at his death, or "the crown of immortality" which Polycarp saw before him; the stripping and "standing in the under garment only" is related of Cyprian at his martyrdom; and Lucian's vulture seems but a parody of the dove which the imaginative piety of Christian legend saw rising from the funeral-pile of Polycarp.* The very year (A.D. 165)

* The dove is omitted in the account given by Eusebius.

of Polycarp's death, which we are distinctly told "was discussed everywhere among the heathen," seems possibly to correspond. Bishop Pearson appears to have considered the whole account as nothing more than a kind of travesty of the martyrdom of Ignatius, and in this idea he has been followed by many German scholars. It has been conjectured that possibly Lucian may have intended to satirise the contempt of death which he speaks of as a characteristic of the Christian sect, and that positive desire for martyrdom which we know from other authorities to have prevailed among some of them to a morbid degree, as a new development of cynicism.

But there seems no good reason to doubt the main accuracy of the account given by Lucian, or to attribute to him any sinister motive in telling the story as he does. The extraordinary fact of this self-immolation of Peregrinus is related, though briefly, by Christian writers —by Tatian, Tertullian, and Eusebius. Aulus Gellius, indeed, speaks of having known him in his earlier life, as living in a cottage in the suburbs of Athens, "a grave and earnest man," to whose wise discourse he had often listened with much pleasure. But a consummate impostor such as Lucian describes may well have succeeded in imposing upon the Roman antiquarian as upon the officers of the Christian Church.* He had

* See Noct. Att., xii. 11. Wieland, all whose remarks on Lucian deserve respect, thought his portrait of Peregrinus manifestly unfair, and wrote a kind of novelette, cast in the form of a Dialogue between Lucian and Peregrinus in Elysium, in which the latter gives a very different account of his life from

probably, as Eusebius relates of him, joined that community for a time, most likely for his own ends, though he may not have held the high position among them which is here ascribed to him. On the motives which led him to the extraordinary act which closed his life, Lucian must have had better opportunities of judging than are open to us; and he plainly considers that he was actuated at first by a fanatical desire for notoriety, and possibly forced at the last to carry out his announcement against his will. It might have required more courage to draw back, in the face of public ridicule and certain exposure, than to brave death amidst the applause of the crowd.

The abuse showered upon Lucian by Christian writers as a "blasphemer" and an "Antichrist" is due partly to his having had ascribed to him a Dialogue called "Philopatris," in which the Christians are maliciously accused of prophesying misfortunes to the state, and which bears internal evidence of having been written by one who had been at some period a member of a Christian Church. As the author of this, they charged him with worse than infidelity—apostasy from the faith, and treason to his former associates. But it has been pretty clearly proved that this work is of much later date, and could not possibly have come from the hand of Lucian. It is true that in his account of the pseudo-prophet Alexander, the only other occasion on which he mentions the Christians by name,

the version here presented to us. There is a good notice of this little work of Wieland's in W. Taylor's 'Historic Survey of German Poetry,' ii. 482.

he has classed them with "atheists and Epicureans;"* but this is only so far as to show that they were all equally incredulous of the pretended miracles of that impostor.

Of the new Kingdom which had risen Lucian had in fact no conception. What opportunities he may have had, or may have missed, of making acquaintance with it, we cannot tell. Its silent growth seems to have been little noted by him. The contempt for death and indifference to riches professed by this new sect would seem to him only echoes of what he had long heard from the lips of those Stoic and Cynic pretenders whom he had made it his special business to unmask; the vagrant preachers of this new faith, supported by contributions, were confounded by him with the half-mendicant professors of philosophy whom he had known too well. He did not care enough about the Christians to hate them much. Their refusal to sacrifice to the national idols—the great testing-point of their martyrs under the reigning emperors—could have been no great crime in the eyes of the author of the "Dialogues of the Gods." Fanaticism in that direction was no worse than fanaticism in the other. His chief attention seems to have been concentrated on that remarkable revival of paganism which began under Hadrian and the Antonines, against which he protests with all the force of a keen intellect and a biting wit. But, far from being the enemy of Christianity, he was, however unintentionally

* "Alexander," 38.

and unconsciously, one of its most active allies. He fought its battle on a totally different ground from its own apologists, and would have been astonished to know that he was fighting it at all; but he was weakening the common enemy. He did the same service to the advancing forces of Christianity as the explosion of a mine does to the storming party who are waiting in the trenches: he blew into ruins the fortifications of pagan superstition, already grievously shaken. He did not know who was to enter in at the breach; but he had a strong conviction that the old stronghold of falsehood ought at any cost not to stand.

END OF LUCIAN.

www.ingramcontent.com/pod-product-compliance
Lightning Source LLC
LaVergne TN
LVHW011228110826
845150LV00006B/1575
* 9 7 8 1 4 2 5 5 1 5 4 0 9 *